OTHER-ESTEEM

OTHER-ESTEEM

Meaningful Life in a Multicultural Society

by

Philip O. Hwang, Ph.D.
University of San Diego

USA	Publishing Office:	ACCELERATED DEVELOPMENT
		A member of the Taylor & Francis Group
		325 Chestnut Street
		Philadelphia, PA 19106
		Tel: (215) 625-8900
		Fax: (215) 625-2940
	Distribution Center:	ACCELERATED DEVELOPMENT
		A member of the Taylor & Francis Group
		7625 Empire Drive
		Florence, KY 41042
		Tel: 1-800-634-7064
		Fax: 1-800-248-4724
UK		ACCELERATED DEVELOPMENT
		A member of the Taylor & Francis Group
		27 Church Road
		Hove
		E. Sussex, BN3 2FA
		Tel: +44 (0) 1273 207411
		Fax: +44 (0) 1273 205612

OTHER-ESTEEM: Meaningful Life in a Multicultural Society

1 2 3 4 5 6 7 8 9 0

Printed by Sheridan Books, Ann Arbor, MI, 2000.
Cover design by Tina Serenshock.
Edited by Hilary Ward and Jim Reed.

A CIP catalog record for this book is available from the British Library.
∞ The paper in this publication meets the requirements of the ANSI Standard Z39.48-1984 (Permanence of Paper)

Library of Congress Cataloging-in-Publication Data

CIP information available from publishers.

ISBN 1-56032-876-2 (paper)

CONTENTS

Preface   ix
Acknowledgments   xi

1 Beyond Self-Esteem   1

Self-Esteem   2
Self-Esteem: The Mythical Cure-All   4
American Reverence of Independence   5
Fast Instant Relief Syndrome   7
The Big Mac Syndrome   9
Habit of Self-Centeredness   11
The "Me" Generation and Self-Esteem   14
Beyond Self-Esteem   14
Mental Blocks to Other-Esteem   16
Other-Esteem   17
We Are Who We Are Because of Others   19
Doses of Other-Esteem   21
Future Challenge: Learn to See the World Anew   21
Key Concepts in This Chapter   22

2 Life from a Different Perspective   23

Power and Source of Our Interpretation   24
Not Just Feeling Better   26
What Color Glasses Are We Wearing?   27
Lives of Fantasy and Illusion   28
Biases Are Based on Distorted Reality   29
Our "Twisted" Minds   30
From Bad Luck to Good Fortune   30
Expanding Our Vision   31

Giving Up Control of Our Lives   32
Three Fundamental Questions of Life   34
Easy Steps to Untainted Perception   34
Change Only What You Can   36
The Choice Is Ours   37
Key Concepts in This Chapter   38

3   **The Conspiracy of Silence**   43

Deaf to Others' Silent Cries   44
Confidentiality: The Glitter and the Tarnish   45
Secrecy Reinforces Negative Behaviors   46
Breaking the Myth of Silence   47
Speak out Now   48
Why We Become Unwilling Co-Conspirators   49
The Courage to Speak Out   50
Break the Silence: The Need to Speak Out   53
Key Concepts in This Chapter   55

4   **Discovering the Inner Ring of Intimacy**   57

Myth and Fantasy About Love   58
"Hello-Goodbye" Marriages and Divorces   59
Disposable Human Beings   59
Joys and Pains of Love   61
Love Alone Is Not Enough   62
All Relationships Can Be Enriching Experiences   63
Change Starts from Within   64
Esteem, Not Competition   65
Plan for Tomorrow's Togetherness Today   66
Togetherness Is First a Frame of Mind   66
Teaching Other-Esteem to Our Children   68
Circles of Support   69
Key Concepts in This Chapter   71

5   **Developing the Ring of Friendship**   73

Mutuality in Life Partnerships   75
Hi-Tech Living   76
Expectation of Self   77

Expectations of Others   78
"Hello-Goodbye" Friendships   79
Pioneering Self-Sufficiency   80
Society of Portable Roots   80
Alone in the Midst of Others   81
Interdependence   82
Sharing Based on Free Choice   82
Steps to Interdependency   84
Developing Our Rings of Support   85
Key Concepts of This Chapter   88

6

Other-Esteem and Leadership   **89**

"Hello-Goodbye" Business   **91**
Key Concepts in This Chapter   **106**

7

Other-Esteem in a Multicultural Society   **107**

Accidents of Life   107
Self Is the Basis of Discrimination   108
The Balance of Self-Esteem and Other-Esteem   109
Examine Self and One's Cultural Background   110
Respect Cultural Differences   111
Valuing and Accepting Others   113
Rights of the Majority   114
The Majority Is Not Always Right   115
Diversity as a Choice and Not a Legal Mandate   117
Networking and Promoting Multiculturalism   120
Key Concepts in This Chapter   121

8

The Psychology of Forgiveness   **123**

Pains and Forgiveness   124
Why Do We Not Forgive?   124
Six Basic Principles of Forgiveness   126
Three Phases of Forgiveness   133
Key Concepts in This Chapter   140

9   **The By-Ways to a Meaningful Life**   143

Personal Wellness Training Program   144
Your Roadmap: The Wheel of Meaningful Life   145
Start Today!   160

References   161
About the Author   163
Index   165

PREFACE

"Dr. Hwang, you have changed my life. I want to personally thank you." These were the words from a total stranger after a speech I gave in Los Angeles. "Several years ago, I attended one of your workshops," she continued. "After the workshop I went home and decided to apply some of the things I learned during the training. My life has changed dramatically, and I am very grateful for your help."

I smiled and thanked the lady for her comments, as there is no greater reward for a lecturer than to hear that what he talks about has a positive impact on someone. I said to her, "I admire you for what you have accomplished. Give yourself credit for what you have done and that you were able to bring back happiness to your life."

This book is written with you in mind. It is a common sense approach to life. It is full of poignant messages for people who are looking for fresh, non-traditional perspectives to life's routine. It is based on a philosophy of inter-dependency vs. independency, mutual cooperation vs. self-sufficiency and synergistic way of action vs. individualistic idiosyncratic behavior.

Many of you are questioning the meaning of life and looking for directions and solutions to relieve your daily stresses and pressures. Hopefully, this short book will result in your leading a happier and more meaningful life.

Learn to see the world anew! This is the challenge as you read through the following pages. You must read this book with great passion, open-mindedness and a desire for change. I am only responsible for what I write. You are responsible for what you get out of it. The extent to which you benefit from the contents of this book depends solely on what you do after you read it.

This book was not written for your enjoyment or entertainment. You must want to learn and change. You must now that you will assimilate at least three things from these pages that help you see life a little differently and learn or re-learn to live a happier life. You must also take responsibility for your own success or failure.

It is my ardent hope that the knowledge gained from my years of experience in teaching, counseling and lecturing, summarized in this book, will help you gain a much clearer perspective of yourself and the kind of life you want. These pages will also help you acquire a better understanding of how you think, why you do the things you do, and the importance of gaining control and direction of your life. These critical avenues to tearing-down inner, limiting walls surrounding the "self," and building many new, strong and sturdy bridges that reach out to families, friends, and the community and even the world at large.

The most fundamental step in change is the realization that the existing order is not working in your life or that there are better alternatives. This book will make a strong case that both of these assessments of our present society are true and that something must be done about them.

Most people are threatened or feel insecure when there is change. Change entails risk, and most of us resist change. Many people believe the wise saying, "no pain, no gain." However, there are some who prefer inaction. You may believe that certain life events will happen and take care of themselves. It follows, then, that if I am attempting to persuade you to change, I must convince you that your present situation can be improved. Fortunately, my task is made much easier by the fact that since you have purchased my book, it is already evident that you are intrigued and are ready to at least consider what I have to say. The true test comes when you start implementing what insights you have gained from these pages.

Read this book with someone significant to you, or find someone special who is also reading this book. The thoughts in these pages are more meaningful when shared, discussed and challenged. When you are finished reading, pass this book on to someone else. Get a color marker, highlight, write and mark your own thoughts and reactions on these pages. This is the intended purpose. Finally, if you are as excited reading it as I am writing it, recommend this book to someone you care about: your colleagues at work, your friends, neighbors, etc. This is the best way to start demonstrating your other-esteem.

ACKNOWLEDGMENTS

First and foremost I want to thank my present and former students. During almost three decades as an educator at different levels, thousands have sat in front of me to acquire new knowledge and skills. They came into my life and impacted me in many different ways. Just as I have touched their lives and changed them. I have grown, matured and learned so much from this relationship. I hope that the majority of them can say the same about this same I-thou encounter with me. Without these students I would not have been a professor. This is a humbling thought. This book would not have been possible. This book is dedicated to all of them: past, present and future seekers of truth and facilitators for a better society.

To all my colleagues and friends at the University of San Diego, my depth of gratitude. Over twenty years many of them have become great friends and wonderful supports in my endeavors.

During the years of writing and re-writing this manuscript, many people have contributed their ideas and suggestions. My sincere heartfelt thanks to Dr. Paula Cordeira, Dean of the School of Education at the University of San Diego. With her strong support and kind encouragement this new revised edition is now a reality. Special thanks also to Shelly Marks, whose contribution to research and editing is invaluable.

My gratitude to Dr. Jon Carlson, for his unwavering support for the concept of Other-Esteem. Thanks to all the wonderful folks at Accelerated Development, especially to Tim Julet and Hilary Ward for their invaluable help in getting this book to print.

Finally, I would like to thank my wife, Joanne, and my two children, Annette and Jonathan, for their love and care. Without them, I would not understand, feel, or appreciate the pain and joy of being a spouse and parent.

Beyond Self-Esteem

No problem can be solved from the same level of consciousness that created it. You must learn to see the world anew.

—Albert Einstein

I once read an interesting parable about the eating arrangements in heaven and hell. In both places, people eat their meals with pairs of six-foot-long chopsticks. The only difference between the diners in heaven and those in hell is that the heavenly folks use the long chopsticks to feed each other across the table, whereas the occupants of hell try desperately to feed themselves with the ungainly utensils—to no avail. The former reaps the rewards of mutual sharing and interdependency, while the latter suffers the consequences of egocentricity and selfishness. This parable points out the benefit and even the necessity of cooperation. It also demonstrates a creative approach to solving a problem and shows the benefit of interdependency.

For the past three decades or so, mental health leaders, speakers, and writers have promoted the self above all else. From the heyday of Individual Sensitivity Training through the Human Potentials movement, from assertiveness training to the self-esteem movement of today, mental health specialists have emphasized and focused almost exclusively on the development and functioning of the self. Each psychological movement has been promoted with fervor, and many people soaked up these precepts, changing their lives and social mores accordingly. These movements have been very successful, but have resulted on a large, social scale in some unexpected and negative results.

Due in large part to the promotion of the self and the derogation of others and social responsibility, we are waking up today to a society on the verge of being consumed by moral decay, devastated by heinous crimes, overtaken by financial greed, and oblivious to social order. Shocked that years of self-promotion have not brought about the happiness or mental equilibrium promised by the gurus of human behavior, there are faint voices questioning the wisdom of a culture based solely on the promotion of self.

☐ Self-Esteem

Self-esteem is often defined as an appreciation of self and self-worth. This acceptance and valuing of self are extremely important in the development of a healthy personality. However, we cannot blame all social ills on the lack of self-esteem, nor can we depend on its promotion as a cure. In fact, too strong a dose of self-esteem may be dangerous.

One illustration of the extent to which self-esteem has been over-emphasized occurred in California. In 1986, the State of California established a special task force to Promote Self-Esteem and Personal and Social Responsibility. After almost four years of study and hearings, the task force concluded that low self-esteem is at the root of many social problems, such as crime, violence, drug and alcohol abuse, academic failure, chronic welfare dependency, child abuse, and teenage pregnancy.

Since this report came out, not just California but the nation as a whole has been caught up in the frenzy of promoting self-esteem. Journals, magazines, and newspapers all publish articles on the topic. Television programs, educational organizations, and political interests have also jumped on the bandwagon. It appears that at least some of the people claiming to be specialists or experts who are teaching self-esteem may even have questionable motives. In addition, many training manuals and books have focused almost entirely on self-esteem and paid little or no attention to the second part of the task force report, namely "personal and social responsibility."

The promotion of personal and social responsibility has been conveniently disregarded. Perhaps it is more expedient and politically correct or modern to talk about self-esteem, and old-fashioned to discuss personal and social responsibility. But to promote self-esteem without advocating personal and social responsibility will result in psychological emptiness and emotional bankruptcy.

Many people who commit crimes of violence possess an unrealistic and exaggerated degree of self-esteem and self-confidence. Their review of research focusing on the relationship between self-esteem and violence led Baumeister, Smart, and Boden (1996) to suggest that high self-esteem is not necessarily a deterrent to violent behavior. Considered by some to be a wake-up call for the psychology community, this research has spurred some overdue critique of the self-esteem movement.

The researchers concluded that overly high self-esteem, when mixed with a threat or challenge to the inflated ego, creates a much stronger recipe for violence than does low self-esteem. Individuals with an extreme degree of self-esteem may have no qualms about knocking others down to lift themselves up. The harm they do to others is of no concern when they seek to prove or protect their own superiority and dominance.

Students in our schools possess a high level of self-esteem compared to other countries. Yet, they also have the highest incidence of violence towards others. In other words, many children care and greatly value themselves and de-value others. Has their exaggerated sense of self-esteem gone to their heads? There are numerous news reports of shocking violence in schools or among youths. Due to their lack of other-esteem, they do not think or feel it wrong to harm others. One teen murders another just for wearing the wrong color jacket. Another is shot over a simple exchange of angry words. The life of another human being has been so devalued as to be worthless in their minds.

In at least some cases, like that of Luke Woodham, a high school student who murdered his mother and two fellow students in Pearl, Mississippi in 1997, psychological assessments have indicated not a lack of self-esteem, but rather narcissistic traits and grandiose self-opinions. In the case of Luke Woodham, a challenge to that inflated self-image had tragic results (Begley, 1998).

Those who head drug empires, gangs, and organized crime syndicates do not lack self-esteem. Baumeister et al. point out that little proof exists in support of the commonly held belief that gang members secretly harbor much self-doubt and insecurity, stating that "violent youths seem sincerely to believe that they are better than other people" (1996, p. 8). It is their arrogance, deluded sense of invincibility, and lack of respect or valuing of others that causes them to commit crimes. It is their sense of superiority that causes them to feel disdain for others who are in any way different from (and, in their minds, inferior to) them. These people have disregarded moral and ethical teachings to seek self-gratification through money, power, and status at a great cost to the rest of society. Where is their personal and social responsibility?

☐ Self-Esteem: The Mythical Cure-All

Many adults entrusted with the care of children often with good intention praise them that they are special and that they can do anything they want to be. These kinds of meaningless statements can actually decrease a child's trust in adults who use them. According to Weissbourd (1996), "The self-esteem movement's constant praising of children is a short cut, a desperate substitute for the inability of teachers and other adults to pay sufficient attention to any one child. But time and attention are real to a child in ways that praise is not" (1996). It is not empty praise, but genuine, meaningful interaction with others that helps children develop a positive sense of self. It takes time and effort, and there are no effective short cuts. Are we willing to do the work it takes?

Tell children they are great and they will be able to accomplish almost anything. This has been the prevailing belief among psychologists, educators, and parents alike, and it has led to a concentrated effort toward boosting students' self-esteem by making them feel that they are lovable and capable, no matter what they do or say. Much time and numerous resources have been spent toward accomplishing this goal. Yet research has time and again shown this approach ineffective. Programs meant to boost self-esteem—described as "a positive, global evaluation of the self"—have failed to result in any notable increase. Furthermore, the actual impact of self-esteem on such matters as violence, drug use, and academic achievement has proven minimal at best (Weissbourd, 1996).

A distinction exists between two types of self-esteem. Global self-esteem, the kind that receives the majority of the attention, is a general sense of pride in oneself not based upon any particular achievement. Earned self-esteem, on the other hand, arises as the result of one's work and accomplishments ("The self-esteem fraud . . .," 1998). Children need opportunities for achievement. It is not enough just to encourage them to feel good about themselves. The inadequacy of this approach is evidenced by the differences in performance between Asian and American youths: studies have shown that despite lower self-evaluations of their academic ability, the Asian elementary school students performed significantly better than the American students, who rated their own abilities much higher ("The self-esteem fraud . . .," 1998).

Our preoccupation with self-esteem, considered by some to be "a national reluctance to grow up" (Kaplan, 1995), has earned the United States criticism internationally. Could it be that we approach the issue from a backward point of view? According to Kaplan, "Competence increases self-esteem, which increases competence." Maybe what we really need is to create standards that give students the chance to increase their competence and encourage them as they build a real foundation for positive self-esteem.

☐ American Reverence of Independence

We Americans have long revered our independence and regard it as an important character trait of our culture. We learned at a very young age that rugged individuals conquered the frontier. Those early settlers were tough, self-sufficient, and self-reliant individuals. The heroes and role models we idealize were often lone rangers who single-handedly accomplished great things without help or cooperation from others. They are, in today's terminology, "self-made" in every sense of the word. We continue this tradition when we rear our children to be independent, self-reliant, self-sufficient, and self-directed.

As the result of our history and culture, we live by a code of stoic individualism, preciously guarding our individuality, determined to do things our own way. There is a subtle social stigma attached to those who depend on others. These people are considered weak, unable to stand on their own feet. Thus, to be independent of others is the ultimate in rugged individualism.

Due to these cultural beliefs in independence and individuality, a major problem for many is the reluctance to ask for help. While we may readily and generously give to others of our time, talent, and money, we may also find it extremely difficult to seek personal help. Consequently, when we need help, we often do not know where to go or how to ask for it. Instead, we continue to deny to ourselves or others that we need it. This is particularly true of those in the helping professions: psychologists, nurses, and doctors. They reach out so readily to others in their jobs, yet find it painfully hard to seek help for their own problems. This is a major problem for many of us who believe in independence and individuality is our reluctance to ask for help. Many of us are very generous with our time, talent, and money; we may readily give to others yet find it extremely difficult to seek personal help.

> The current social paradigm enthrones independence.
> —*Stephen Covey (1989)*

Our illusion of self-importance often prevents us from learning from others who have succeeded in areas where we have failed. However, we need to learn from history. It teaches us that those who refuse to change and adapt to new situations and circumstances will eventually fall. Consider the failures of the Roman Empire, the decline of the Greek Civilization, and the collapse of Ming and Qing dynasties in China. Each great civilization declined because its leaders and citizens refused to see and adapt to social demands for change. Without a willingness to see life events differently and a readiness for needed change and improvement, a whole culture and society will begin to stagnate, deteriorate, and even collapse. Soon, other societies—younger, stronger, and more able to adapt—will supersede the old. If we continue to refuse to adapt to new situations, American culture may also earn a place in history on the list of past giants.

In order for American society to reclaim its social order and promote harmony, it is vital that we, as parents, educators, and leaders, rear our children to understand the importance of sharing, cooperation, mutual respect, and interdependence. We all need to learn that the whole of the community is greater than the sum of each of its individual members.

Our childhood idols and today's role models are often rock singers, popular athletes, movie and television stars, political leaders, or successful business executives. What we admire about them are their personal conquests. In today's society, personal success is judged on the basis of the number of wins versus losses. We are expected to be as good as the best and better than the rest. We have an obsession for ranking our leaders, heroes, products, services, and even academic institutions by popularity polls. We are so achievement-oriented that all we want is to be regarded or worshipped as the best, as Number One.

Hero worship should be as outdated as royalty and empires. It was useful once upon a time. In medieval times, hero worshippers and subjects of royalty were obedient and non-questioning people living a very simple life. Today, we hear, see, and know more about our heroes and leaders than ever before, often more than they want us to know. We challenge their values, question their behavior, and even dispute their decisions. We are better educated and not as powerless as generations past. We no longer follow blindly or obey without independent judgment.

How often have we been disappointed or shocked by stories of popular role models once held in high esteem by the general public?

American culture focuses primarily on role models from the entertainment and sports worlds, yet these people are among the most unpredictable in terms of their behavior. They often do not conduct themselves according to what they preach. Many of them enlist public relations firms to present a glorified image to the public. We often are shocked and angry when the truth leaks out. This kind of hero-worshipping is irresponsible. It diminishes individual initiative, takes away personal responsibility, and sets up unrealistic expectations. How much better to view a role model as one that inspires us to do what is good and right for everyone, that feeds us with examples, opens our minds to new ideas, and broadens our views as to what can be. The challenge is for us to set up a different, more balanced, and healthier model.

☐ Fast Instant Relief Syndrome

In addition to American culture's distinctive reverence for independence, a second characteristic trait is the passion for immediate gratification or instant relief from any emotional or physical discomfort. This I call the "Fast Instant Relief Syndrome," or "FIRES" for short.

A quick glance at the diverse communities we live in shows just how deeply the FIRES mentality has wormed its way into our daily lives. Instant noodles, two-minute parenting, quick weight reductions, fast-acting medicines, "dinner served in ten minutes or it's free," thirty-minute pizza delivery, get-rich-quick schemes, and psychic healers hanging out shingles that promise to "solve all your problems in one visit." We cannot deny it. We are an impatient society.

As we bustle about our daily lives, we try to convince ourselves that we are extremely busy and efficient people. Many of us now seek efficiency over meaning of our actions. A good example is our love affair with fast food. Some of us feel so short of time that we do not even take time to eat lunch. Instead, we are willing to pay someone to deliver a take-out meal. When the food arrives, we wolf it down while continuing to work at our desks.

Why are Americans in such a hurry? Why are we always so short of time? Everyone seems to be in a hurry and trying very hard to save time. Yet everyone in the world, from babies to senior citizens, from the rich to the poor, has the same 24-hour day.

How many hours or minutes have you saved up to now? Where have you deposited the time you saved? With our whole society geared toward saving time, what are you doing with all the extra time you have on your hands?

As I pondered these questions, another thought hit me. If we have so many ingenious ways to save time, and are doing more and more tasks in less and less time, are we more efficient or productive than other countries, and does this mean that we are more and more satisfied with ourselves because of our productivity? Dare I also suggest that we are happier and more contented with life too? The answer is an emphatic "No." For all our bustling around, we do not have more time on our hands. We are not any more productive or efficient than others. There are many other countries whose productivity is much higher per capita than ours.

We live in a society where time is a precious commodity and everyone is searching for ways to save it or use it more efficiently. Most of us are so caught up in the hurried-up syndrome that we are not aware of how our lifestyle affects us and our society. We have invented so many human conveniences to satisfy our hunger for instant satisfaction. We now secure our shoes with Velcro strips, receive money from a dispensing machine, talk and listen to computers, and get an instant tan by going to a tanning salon.

American society is commonly perceived around the world as a society that expects and demands instant gratification. Foreigners coming to the United States for the first time are often astounded by all the fast food restaurants with drive-through service and the proliferation of frozen microwave dinners. Everything seems to be geared towards saving time and effort. A good friend of mine who came from Sweden to do her graduate studies in San Diego commented that only in the United States can you find so many varieties of instant frozen foods. More than just fast food restaurants and frozen microwave dinners, our whole society is obsessed with the need to save time. My Swedish friend pointed out how much of our precious time we spend in automobiles. With drive-through banking, drive-through restaurants, instant film developing shops, and car phones, we can eat, bank, and work without ever leaving our cars.

American custom dictates that one always be on time for appointments and for social events. Many cultures have differing perspectives. For some countries, it is more socially correct to be a little late when you are invited to someone's home for dinner. It would be considered rude if you arrived early or even on time.

This fixation on time is a symptom of our outlook on life. We are a society full of short-sighted individuals who are used to instant gratification or getting a "quick fix." We have new ideas, technology, and information thrown at us at an amazing pace, and in order to cope, we rush ourselves to keep up. Then we come to expect that the rest of the environment and those around us, those who provide us with products and services, to keep up with that pace, and the effect of those around us rushing to keep up makes us rush more and more.

☐ The Big Mac Syndrome

Going back briefly to our fast-food analogy, American society has become an "eat-on-the-run" culture. We are caught up in the "Big Mac Syndrome." The Big Mac Syndrome is actually a part of a vicious cycle: the pace of our world and the fast-changing technology give us less time to adjust, less time to think, and actually less leisure time than in the pre-technological age. In any event, because of the pace, we rush to and from and in between, and the Big Mac Syndrome is both a cause and effect of this pace. Ray Kroc, the founder of McDonald's, understood the impatient nature of the American people. The Big Mac hamburger is prepared instantly as we order. The satisfaction of our hunger is just as immediate, as we consume the hamburger in matter of minutes. This is a syndrome many of us have acquired. Human socialization and interaction that used to come with dining are becoming extinct in our fast food society. People who go to fast-food chains often go alone. If they are with another person, because of the perceived need to rush, the conversations they have are often as quick, shallow, and devoid of substance as the food they are gulping down. Eating is a biological necessity. But dining is a social event. What originally was supposed to be a "break" for a mini social event is turning out to be just another fast, instant relief of human physiological need.

We live searching for instant gratification, especially when we are hungry. We want to be relieved of our hunger pangs RIGHT NOW. And this demand for instant gratification has spilled over to other aspects of our lives as well.

Technological advances have made it possible for us to work more efficiently, solve problems better and even pay our taxes faster. Advances in telecommunications allow us to communicate instantaneously with people all over the world. Overnight delivery services, satellite communications, and fax machines enable us to speed information around the globe in a matter of seconds.

Yet, we are still not satisfied. Look at how often corporate America upgrades or changes its computer hardware and software. Instead of being grateful for the technology we have, we impatiently pine for newer, faster and more sophisticated machines with greater memory storage. We complain when we do not have the latest and the most up-to-date equipment and programs.

The Big Mac Syndrome is not just about our eating habits, but about our whole lifestyle. Sociologists say we can identify a culture by the food it exports to other countries. America certainly has exported a lot of fast or junk food. What does this say about the American culture?

If this pace is maintained, heartburn will not be the only problem we will have to deal with.

Most people are patient and willing to stay in line to obtain things they really want and treasure. This, in some way, is a reflection of people's values and culture. Here in America, we do not line up for anything except rock concerts, rides at amusement parks, and sporting events. We are willing to be patient for these things because entertainment is a big part of American society. However, we do not have patience for most other matters.

During a visit to Moscow, I could not believe my eyes when I saw the long line outside a McDonald's. Our guide said that it takes about three hours to buy a McDonald's hamburger in Moscow. Muscovites could not obtain beef in the grocery stores, so they came to McDonald's to purchase a hamburger. How many Americans would wait three hours in front of a fast food restaurant to buy a hamburger?

We presume that to be served first and immediately is our right. It is others' responsibility to make sure that happens. If it does not, we complain and make life miserable for all involved. This kind of attitude makes life very stressful for all of us.

Is American culture full of individualistic satisfaction and uncontrolled impatience, without regard for others? Can we conclude that American culture is primarily one of individual entertainment and instant gratification? The answer is definitely "Yes!"

In our constant rush toward the quick fix, some of us have even lost the skills for meeting and relating to people—so we put ads in local papers or on videotapes to hurry things up. We do not know how to enjoy a natural human necessity—sleep—so we take pills to put us to sleep quickly.

It should also stand to reason that if we can obtain meals in moments, solve business problems with labor-saving, high-tech computers, and communicate instantly through fax machines and international phones, we ought to have far more time to relax, take a break, and "mellow out," "chill," or "veg," as our teenage children tell us. (This time they are right.)

If we truly want to loosen up, what is the first step? The best possible advice comes from nature: there are no shortcuts. "Instant" may be all right for noodles, but it certainly has no place in the world of business, social, or personal relationships. It takes time to grow a beautiful rose garden, nourish a majestic redwood to reach the sky, or cultivate a field sprinkled with multi-colored wildflowers. It takes time to get to know and understand other people, to establish a meaningful relationship, to build a future together. It takes time and patience to raise children with love, support, understanding, and a willingness to let them choose their own course. So slow down and kick back for a little while. Think about all your friendships and relationships and prepare yourself for a more enjoyable and meaningful life.

☐ Habit of Self-Centeredness

Infants and children grow up thinking only of themselves. Their world revolves around immediate needs and wishes. As we mature, we too often continue to place our own needs above the needs of others. We continue to believe that it is acceptable to be self-centered, and that our individual happiness is the most important goal in life. Many of our role models—teachers, parents, friends, and relatives—also seem to follow the same creed.

Minds that are clouded by self-obsession will remain stagnant and unquestioning. Our vision of the world around us can become narrow and prejudiced. Ignorance, refusal to face reality, or simply the lack of critical thought can easily build up mental barriers. Most of us accept what we see and hear as the truth and rarely stop to question its validity. For years, psychologists have told us that we should be looking only after Number One—the self. So long as Number One is happy, nothing else seems to matter. As a result, many of us make choices based on what's in it for the self without considering the consequences our choices have on others.

The balance between individual choice and social responsibility is an extremely delicate one. It is a conflict with-in the self—between the assumptions of personal rights and the demands of individual responsibility. This struggle to maintain equilibrium is a continuous one and often increases with social dictates of the time. The recent social changes in attitude over smoking in public present a good example. In the early 1980s, few would have predicted that America in the nineties would ban smoking in so many places. But we now have smoke-free restaurants, factories, office buildings, and even casinos. Airlines have banned smoking on all their domestic flights and some international routes. Societal demands

> Events in life always provide a choice. This choice should be based on meaning or purpose in one's life.
> —*Phil Hwang*

for healthier air supersede individual rights and the choice to smoke in these areas.

Just as societal choices invariably have consequences for everyone, individual freedom is never absolute. It always comes with some personal relinquishment. With growing concerns over crime in our streets, Congress passed a crime bill a few years ago. Among other things, this bill takes away the individual's right to purchase and own assault rifles. What is the ideal balance between the rights of self and the needs of society?

In almost every aspect of our lives, there exist possible conflicting individual goals and group interests. Our present day legal system offers us some prime examples of the promotion of individual interests rather than personal and social responsibility. How often we have heard that a certain company has been fined thousands or even millions of dollars for infractions of the law, yet the company does not admit any wrong-doing? If there is no wrong-doing, why the penalty? If there is acceptance of the punishment, why not of the responsibility? It seems many of us understand truth and responsibility, but few of us are willing to abide by them. We are willing to bear the responsibility only after we are caught and found guilty. Otherwise, many people continue to protest their innocence.

The pleading of any defendant is guilt or innocence, and not truth or falsehood. One determines guilt according to the laws of the state or nation. How many of us understand the ramifications and intricacies of our laws in order to make rational decisions? Or are we at the mercy of a complicated legal system to interpret for us what is right and what is wrong? Guilt is also a state of conscience and is based on the moral capacity or value orientation of the individual to make a judgment. Society advocates certain moral norms and dictates of values and customs. What are our present norms and dictates of civilities? Have our levels of moral and social standards and responsibilities deteriorated since the framing of the Constitution by our forefathers? Have we taken up the causes of the individual at the expense of society?

Perhaps the best example of the conflict between individual goals and social objectives can be found by observing the actions of some professional athletes in this country. Most of the highest paid people in the world are professional athletes who often jump from team to team in search of bigger contracts with sky-high salaries. What happened to teamwork, team loyalty, fans, and city-connectedness? Professional athletes are not rewarded for their teamwork or loyalty. They are recognized for their individual achievements. Thus, on many of our professional teams are selfish individuals seeking personal glorification and excessive payment. There is great irony in this situation. All team sport players are mutually dependent on their teammates in order to win. Can the star pitcher alone win the World Series? He needs at least eight other players. Ironically, in order for the professional athletes to achieve their personal and individual goals, they have to embrace teamwork and cooperation.

A few years ago, the major league baseball players went on strike. After months of half-hearted negotiation, the owners' and players' representatives could not come to an agreement. The entire season, including the World Series, was canceled. Is this strike the result of individualistic millionaires who do not understand or believe in human interdependency?

Historically, a strike was a weapon utilized in the labor movement to protect the average wage earner and to help him obtain higher wages and/or better working conditions. The baseball strike came down to a battle between two groups of the super-rich to add more millions to their bank accounts. As a consequence, it caused extreme hardships for thousands of wage earners who depended on the game to make a living. Did these super-wealthy athletes, in their struggle for fairness and justice, ever consider the injustice and unfairness they have inflicted on those who are dependent on them to put bread on their dinner table?

While life's abundance has a tendency to exaggerate or blur our perception of needs, wants, likes, and dislikes, freedom to choose can sometimes be limited by availability of supply. During one of my many trips to the People's Republic of China, I heard a woman in my group ask a waiter for a bottle of caffeine-free Diet Coke. The waiter understood "Coke," so he brought her a bottle of regular Coke, the only kind they had. She shrugged her shoulders, smiled, and drank it anyway.

How many of us have been fooled by promotions and advertisements that cater to our egos? "Have it your way," says Burger King. So you go in to a Burger King restaurant and say to the attendant, "I want my Whopper on a bagel." Would you have it your way? Of course not! The truth is that there is no absolute individuality and freedom. Choices are always limited, whether you realize it or not.

Warehouse stores, designer outlets, and discount stores have popped up all over the United States, offering Americans a multitude of choices at bargain prices on everything from potato chips to blue jeans to appliances. However, customers at these establishments may have to spend time digging through racks and bins to find what they want, bag their own groceries, and do without some of the extra help they might find at more expensive supermarkets or department stores. Yet many people opt for the lower prices these stores offer at the expense of the service provided by some of their more pricey counterparts. That is an individual choice. These are the gives and takes of life. There are no absolutes.

In our society of give and take, there is a price for personal freedom and individuality. There is also a high cost for social order and civility. This is the principle of interdependency. Understanding the importance and power of human interdependency is one of the most meaningful lessons we need to learn in life, and it offers us a better understanding of our attitudes towards others.

The "Me" Generation and Self-Esteem

The 1980s belonged to the "Me" generation. It was an era where it was socially acceptable and politically correct to be selfish and self-serving. Individual needs and desires superseded the needs of the family, community, and society. Divorce and children from broken families were no longer the exception—they became the norm. Drugs, crime, and violence became major problems in our large cities. Even more frightening, the social problems began to reach beyond the cities. No town or community was immune to drug traffic or gang activity anymore.

Gangs and gang violence have spread throughout the country, and gang-related violence has claimed an increasing number of lives. We only have to read our newspapers to become aware of the host of problems that our society faces. Violence, rape, and theft are all crimes against others. We have placed ourselves, our needs, and our wants above other people. We have taken self-esteem to a dangerous extreme, and it may be backfiring on us. Again, Roy Baumeister and colleagues (1996, p. 8) said: "What would work better for the country is to forget about self-esteem and focus on self-control."

By our actions and by our words, we—in our homes, schools, communities, and corporations—have to transmit to the next generation that extreme individualism (and all its pitfalls) is no longer a social mandate. We need to learn to see the world anew. We need to promote a new order of balance between the self and others.

Beyond Self-Esteem

Webster's Dictionary has hundreds of entries with the word "self" hyphenated: self-image, self-governing, self-sufficient, etc. Not a single word, however, is hyphenated with "other." Does this not tell us something about our culture? After all, language is a form of communication and a reflection of our society. This clearly indicates that we are truly obsessed with the self and not concerned enough with others.

I would like to make a strong case for promoting personal and social responsibility. It is even more vital than promoting self-esteem, and would help us to attain a healthy balance of self and other for a more fulfilling life for all of us.

We attain self-esteem from social values and expectations learned through our various relationships at different levels. Since we are all connected to our society through these direct or indirect linkages with others, it is crucial that we now look at a new

> **Self-esteem must be balanced with other-esteem. This is the resulting synergy of Yin-Yang.**
> *—Phil Hwang*

term that describes our relationship with society. I would like to be so bold as to coin a new word for Mr. Webster: "other-esteem."

Our obsession with ourselves needs to be tempered by focusing more on others and the communities in which we live. We must shift from self-esteem to other-esteem. Instead of always looking out for Number One, we need to look out for each other.

The basis for developing a healthy other-esteem is to watch out for each other without the expectation of reward or compensation. Another way to perceive other-esteem is through the perspective of relationships. Positive and effective human relationships are essential to our well being. These human contacts keep us alive. They bring us joy and happiness. They encourage us to become productive and grow to reach our fullest potential. In living a life of mutual dependency, we enhance our individual ego while learning from and encouraging others.

In the last decade, the movement toward a concept of others has begun to gain acceptance in this country. The legacies of the 1980s included the crash of the stock market, escalating violence, and an increasing number of dysfunctional families. But there are indications of some changes. Many Americans are beginning to reevaluate their lives and their role in society. Today, the baby boomer generation, for example, is asking, "Are money and status all I want from life?" Newspapers report of families moving away from big cities to the easier and simpler life of smaller towns. Others have moved away from careers in often stressful, competitive corporate life to become personal entrepreneurs working out of their homes.

These changes, however, merely affect external factors and serve only as "Band-Aid" approaches to life's problems. Stresses and problems follow us around. Small towns are no longer safe havens from crime. True solutions are found within, and only personal changes can bring about the desired effect.

As the concept of other-esteem takes root and spreads throughout society, people will begin to see more clearly that in the long run, most social objectives and individual goals do converge. Through an increased awareness of our interdependence with others, our horizons will expand to include not just ourselves, but those around us as well. A quick survey of society yields many situations where other-esteem can bridge the gap between individual goals and social fear. When burglary decreases, we will experience less violation of our rights to ownership. These changes will not happen without our belief in human interdependency, pervasive understanding, acceptance, and respect for one another.

Our daily behavior must reflect a constant concern and caring for the people around us. Everyday acts and daily habits can build a sense of community and connectedness with one another (Flaubert, 1997). We are seeing more caring for the homeless, heightened awareness towards educating and helping substance abusers, less fear of and more assistance for those suffering from AIDS, and a greater generosity towards disaster victims around the world. These signs indicate that American society is moving away from an "I" society to a "We" society. It is said that Dr. Martin Luther King, Jr. often asked his followers and listeners to tell him what they had done for others. It is a question that we would all do well to consider.

☐ Mental Blocks to Other-Esteem

The following behaviors may be some of the reasons for our lack of degree of practicing other-esteem:

- Culture of individualism and self-sufficiency
- Reverence for extreme independence
- Belief in superlatives—being the best, Number One
- Society's reward of individual accomplishment
- Fast Instant Relief Syndrome
- Focus on causes and not on consequences
- Favoring individual rights over social responsibility
- Low level of tolerance toward others' perceived shortcomings
- Giving into emotion over reason

☐ Other-Esteem

Other-esteem is the respect, acceptance, caring, valuing, and promotion of all human beings, without reservation. Promotion of other-esteem is that much more difficult in our present day of diversity and multiculturalism. It is not just kindness toward a few—most of us practice this. It is kindness towards all: any gender, race, lifestyle, socioeconomic status, etc. Any practice of kindness is admirable, and this world can use more of it. Sometimes, however, acts of kindness stem from personal guilt, anticipation of reward, social pressures, a hidden political agenda, or even a personal superiority complex.

> Other-esteem is the respect, acceptance, caring, valuing, and promoting of all human beings.
> —*Phil Hwang*

Other-esteem starts with a state of mind. It is a mental attitude that truly accepts the equality of all people. It does not look down on others because they are less wealthy, less socially connected, from another neighborhood, or of a different skin color, gender, or lifestyle. In other words, other-esteem puts one equal to others—not above others, regardless of appearances and circumstances.

Next, other-esteem is a high degree of respect, understanding and tolerance of other people who may think, believe, feel, and behave differently. It is not merely an altruistic demonstration of kindness or generosity towards those who are less fortunate than we are. Other-esteem demands respect, acceptance, and valuing without conditions. It is also a realization and acceptance of the fact that we live in an interdependent world, and that interaction with and dependence on other human beings are not signs of weakness or inferiority. These behaviors are reflections of strength and a higher level of human functioning.

Every individual should possess a healthy balance of both self-esteem and other-esteem. The two are not diametrically opposed; in fact, they complement each other. Self is incomplete without the Other. Self is empty without the Other. Self is lonely without the Other.

There are different facets of other-esteem (see Figure 1.1). These facets are not necessarily reached in progression. Various situations and circum-

> The self is incomplete without the other. The self is empty without the other. The self is lonely without the other.
> —*Phil Hwang*

stances in different personal relationships will dictate the appropriate response. We do not have to demand that one always act on all the different facets of other-esteem at all times. This is not humanly

1. *Non-offensive*. Other-esteem is, by definition, positive. This is the first and most basic step on the ladder to other-esteem. Thus, no offensive conduct can ever be tolerated. No physical or verbal abuse. No pranks, insults, or put-downs. Definitely no violent, aggressive, or destructive behaviors. This is the least we can do in our life with others so our presence is welcomed. Are you the cause of pain to anyone?

2. *Friendly*. We must be neighborly, amicable and sociable, not individualistic or egotistical. We have friends, colleagues and associates with whom we interact, have fun and relate on a personal level. Do you seek to establish and maintain friendships with others?

3. *Courteous*. Common social courtesy is to be practiced. For example, there is a "Thank you!" to the waiter when food is served. There is no cutting in front of others waiting in line, no interrupting others just to hear one's own voice. There is also no self-righteous blowing one's own horn. Rudeness has no place in society. How courteous are you?

4. *Kind*. Kindness is helping others in need. It shows that we have a good heart when we do nice things for others without expecting anything in return. Kindness is most evident during Thanksgiving and Christmas holidays, but we need to realize that every day we have something to be thankful for and reasons to be kind to others. How have you expressed your kindness lately?

5. *Respectful*. Respect is the expression of regard for someone, an admiration and reverence for who the person is and not what he or she stands for. If we respect others, we will in turn receive their respect. Are you selective in your demonstration of respect?

6. *Accepting*. Develop the ability to acknowledge and to welcome others' individual, social, and cultural uniqueness. "Individual difference" is a two-way street. For our idiosyncrasies to be accepted by others, we must learn to understand and accept the uniqueness of others. Acceptance of others involves our ability to perceive life from others' viewpoint. How do you show your acceptance of others?

7. *Valuing*. Treasure and prize relationships with others. We admire and revere the richness of others' personality, and do nothing to jeopardize this interdependence. This valuing is based on the fact that we are who we are because of others. I am an author only because you are a reader. I am a professor only because over the years there have been students in my classes. This is a very humbling realization of interdependence. To what extent do you acknowledge and show your appreciation of others' contribution in your life?

8. *Praising*. Cheer others on. Be sincerely happy for their little successes and great achievements. Praise them and praise them often. Others need to know that we appreciate their efforts and accomplishments, regardless of whether these efforts affect our own lives. Surprise

others often with praise rather than negative criticism. How often do you praise others' efforts?

9. *Promoting Others.* There is no greater degree of other-esteem than the unselfish promotion of others. To promote others, we help them achieve new heights in their careers, support their efforts, and mentor their progress. We foster their causes, ideas, and principles without jealousy or competition. Have you helped others fulfill their needs or wants?

10. *Forgiving.* Of all the levels of other-esteem, this is the most difficult and challenging to achieve. Can we forgive someone who has hurt us and get on with our lives? We can and we must! (See Chapter 8.) Have you forgiven those who have caused you pain?

FIGURE 1.1.   Ten facets of other-esteem.

possible, or even necessary. When we decide to take the road to other-esteem, the most important point to remember is that just being nice to everybody is not enough. Other-esteem requires more than just being non-offensive. We must learn to expand to all the facets of other-esteem.

Other-esteem makes one more humble than proud and more cooperative than competitive. We have learned self-esteem from life experiences; we can acquire other-esteem from similar life experiences. It is possible and necessary to change our perspective. We must recognize that our lives consist of a series of complex, interrelated, and intricate relationships. Our relationships and interactions with others spin out around us like a spider's web; our individual actions and words may have a far-reaching effect on others. The more we go out of our way to understand, respect, accept, and promote others, the better we will feel about ourselves and the more balanced and healthy our lives will be. Increasing our degree of other-esteem will complete the self, making the self "whole."

☐ We Are Who We Are Because of Others

> The self is synergized by the other. The self is complimented by the other. The self is enriched by the other.
> —*Phil Hwang*

Leaders are only leaders as long as there are followers. Generals are commanders only because there are soldiers to carry out their orders.

The president of a company is the boss because there are employees who listen and who follow the company's policies, mission, and vision. Furthermore, the success of leaders of any organization or country relies on the quality achievements and dedicated service of their followers.

In our professional and personal lives, we each have unique and specific roles to play: sometimes as the leader, sometimes as the follower. Whichever role we choose to play, there are always others who will take up different roles. We must learn how to interact in a healthy balance with them. We cannot live solely by ourselves, nor are we personally complete without others. There is a feeling of emptiness. We are mutually dependent on each other, and all of us have a profound effect on the attitudes and behaviors of the people around us (see Figure 1.2).

Throughout the book you will find these simple self-checks of your attitudes and actions regarding the issues discussed in the text. They are designed to test and increase your self-awareness of these issues. For each question, circle your answer on a scale of 1 to 5, with 1 representing "Always" and 5 representing "Never."

	Always				Never
1. I respect and accept all races and cultures.	1	2	3	4	5
2. I understand and value individual differences.	1	2	3	4	5
3. I believe in and practice interdependency.	1	2	3	4	5
4. I choose mutual cooperation over competition.	1	2	3	4	5
5. I listen more and talk less.	1	2	3	4	5
6. I am open to new attitudes and beliefs in my life.	1	2	3	4	5
7. I truly believe that there is always an alternative.	1	2	3	4	5
8. I mentor subordinates and support colleagues.	1	2	3	4	5
9. I focus on team success over personal gain.	1	2	3	4	5
10. I prefer consensus to majority rule.	1	2	3	4	5
11. I seek solutions rather than reasons for failures.	1	2	3	4	5
12. I promote the personal and social interest of others.	1	2	3	4	5

FIGURE 1.2. Simple check of your other-esteem.

☐ **Doses of Other-Esteem**

To counteract the distorted perception of life based on the goal of total self-sufficiency, we need to acquire a healthy dose of *other-esteem*, a new attitude and practice towards life in relation with others. The attainment of individual goals and the fulfillment of social responsibilities can be balanced by encouraging and fostering the growth of other-esteem in American society. Life is much more than just a competitive game to see who is better, richer, stronger, smarter, and more successful. Wealth, strength, intelligence, and success do not guarantee satisfaction in life. Life is about caring, sharing, relationships, and happiness. Because our lives are interwoven with the lives of other people through a complex network of relationships, our success or failure can affect many others. Thus, we should make our choices and decisions only after considering the implications and potential consequences for others. Through cooperation and sharing, everyone can achieve their goals and happiness.

As the concept of other-esteem takes root and spreads throughout society, people will begin to see more clearly that in the long run, most social objectives and individual goals do converge. Through an increased awareness of our interdependence with others, our horizons will expand to include not just ourselves, but those around us. A quick survey of society yields many situations where other-esteem can bridge the gap between individual goals and social objectives. When violence in our streets is curtailed, we will regain our freedom to travel without fear. When burglary and robbery decrease, we will experience less violation of our rights to ownership. These changes will not happen without our belief in human interdependency, pervasive understanding, acceptance, and respect for one another.

☐ **Future Challenge:**
Learn to See the World Anew

We can all change our focus from self to a balanced life that includes self and other. How do we go about making that shift? How do we maintain a balance of caring for self while demonstrating high esteem for others? The following are challenges and issues that will be explored in subsequent chapters in this book.

• We must learn to accept the basic principle that the self alone is insufficient and incomplete. The self can fulfill and complete itself only through meaningful relationships with others.

- We need to understand how we are the way we are, and how we think, feel, and act differently from as well as similarly to others. Then we must re-examine and challenge our present prevailing attitudes, values, and beliefs.
- We need to listen and learn from people of different perspectives. Many of us have mastered the skill of talking. Now we must learn to master the art of listening.
- We have to understand and believe that our own self-esteem is enhanced by the efforts and successes of any group or unit we belong to: family, church, sports teams, school, company, city, country, etc. Learn from new life experiences to see life in a more balanced view of the self-other continuum.
- We must learn to share ourselves with others. There are people all around us who need our support in so many different ways. And we need others just as they need us. We need to develop our own personal support system.
- In every endeavor, we must learn to perform and function as a team.

☐ Key Concepts in This Chapter

1. American culture focuses on the self, independence, and self-sufficiency.
2. The Self is lonely, incomplete, and empty without the Other.
3. Self-esteem must be balanced with other-esteem.
4. Other-esteem is the acceptance, respect, valuing, and promoting of others.
5. We are who we are because of others.
6. The balance of social objectives and personal goals can be achieved through the balance of self-esteem and other-esteem, each of which enhances the other.

Life from a Different Perspective

"Man is not disturbed by the things that happened, but by the perception of the things that happened."

—Confucius

Picture a very common scene: it is morning rush hour. The roads are clogged and congested with commuters. You are stopped at a red light, deep within your own thoughts. When the light turns green, you are a little slow to react. Immediately, the driver behind you blasts his horn, which only serves to startle and embarrass you. As the traffic begins to move, you hear a sudden screeching sound and see the same driver, no longer behind you, but now beside you in the fast lane, giving you an angry stare and saluting you with what I call the "half-a-peace sign." An example of road rage?

Now, most people would consider this to be an obscene and insulting action. They most likely will immediately throw up their finger, repeating the same gesture. This exchange frequently leads to confrontations complete with verbal abuse, automobile accidents, fist fights, or even an occasional tragic shooting. All because someone wanted to gain a single second at a stop light. Since I perceive it to be "half a peace sign," I smile at him, wave my hand, and drive on.

The power is always within us to retain the way we think and select interpretation about events affecting us. Dr. Viktor Frankl, in his classic book, *Man's Search for Meaning* (1984), described how he kept his sanity and will to live during the Second World War, through the torture and murder of his entire family at the concentration camps.

Dr. Frankl valued the sanctity and integrity of the human mind. No one could desecrate or destroy it. Just like the great ancient Chinese sage, Confucius, Dr. Frankl understood the power of the mind to see and to interpret external events.

☐ Power and Source of Our Interpretation

To attain other-esteem, we must learn to interpret life from a different perspective. Nothing comes to us except through our perception. This is our window to the outside world. The mind is the most powerful and important part of the human body. Learning to understand the human thought process and to be able to interpret thoughts and perceptions differently are among the most meaningful tasks in the human maturation process.

Most of us are not aware of the powerful influence that our minds have over our feelings and lives. Knowledge of the thinking process enables us to gain insight into how our thinking patterns critically influence our feelings and direct our behavior.

We often say "That is just the way I am" or "I grew up that way and there is nothing I can do about it." But that is not true. Change is possible for everyone, and it starts with our own perception of life. Heather Whiteston, deaf from childhood, overcame tremendous odds to be chosen Miss America of 1995. She said during an interview that the most handicapped person in the world is a negative thinker.

We may think of ourselves as independent, creative, and very happy with our ability to live our own life and pursue our career. In reality, however, society, the workplace, family, friends, churches, customs, and traditions dictate and influence a great deal of our thoughts, feelings, and behaviors. We treasure and practice our freedom, but at times fail to grasp that it has severe limitations. We demand personal rights, but do not understand or are unwilling to accept the responsibilities that accompany these rights. We often act or react on our emotional instincts and then are shocked at the natural and logical consequences

> Man is not disturbed by the things that happened but by the perception of things that happened.
>
> —*Confucius*

that follow. Our minds often react to specific external event and we make a choice that we later regret and wonder why or how we could have made such a stupid decision.

If we want to view life from a different perspective, it is very important that we thoroughly assess what is stored inside the hard disk of our mind. It is one thing to say that we can interpret things in any way we want; it is another to question how we make our decisions. The following questions might help us understand better how we interpret external events and how we respond to them.

- Based on what relevant data do we compare and evaluate our internal or external stimuli?
- Are these data based on reality as experienced in our society today?
- Are our decisions predicated solely on our personal desires and benefits?
- How often do we consider the consequences of our behavior on others?
- Are there better alternatives?
- Think out of the box or think without the box at all.

Our point of view, however, can no longer be solely from the self perspective. We have to start seeing from others' points of view. Nobody can live a life based on erroneous or outmoded assumptions. The ability to accomplish certain tasks may not be reason enough for one to proceed with the decision or a particular course of action.

The ancient Romans believed there was nothing they could not accomplish given enough planning and human engineering. But the larger question besides whether or not a task can be accomplished is whether or not is should be undertaken in the first place. The popular movie *Jurassic Park*, in which scientists cloned dinosaurs from ancient DNA with disastrous results, raised this issue. Before asking how an experiment should be conducted, they should first ask whether it should be conducted at all. Scientists should ask why an experiment should even be performed. What are their purposes? What are they trying to achieve? What is the likely outcome for the individual as well as the society? There are ethical considerations and questions that should be asked about

> Law of Effective Communication: I am responsible for what I say but not what you hear.
>
> —*Phil Hwang*

how and why events and tasks are initiated or approached. It is best to ask about the long and short range consequences of our actions, not only for ourselves but also for others and the environment. How will this help? Whom will this hurt? Are the advantages outweighed by the costs to self and others?

Mental attitude or perception is everything, and our interpretations of various life events of human interactions must be based on a balance of self-esteem and other-esteem. Our society, however, does not function from the perspective of other-esteem.

☐ Not Just Feeling Better

One of my friends who works in the entertainment industry and has ample opportunities to observe people from all different backgrounds once commented to me, "You know, most people don't think." This comment surprised me and I asked him to elaborate. My friend believes the majority of people he comes into contact with do not really sit back and think about life and what it means to them. Most of the time we accept what others say to us and rarely question the consequences of our actions or lack of any response.

Some people in our society are in the auto-pilot or cruise control mode most of the time. If we want to, we do not have to exert any effort; life is a smooth ride. In order to combat cognitive distortion, we must turn off the auto-pilot switches in our heads, disengage the cruise control, and take full charge of our life. We must think clearly where we are going and how we are going to arrive at our destination. As the saying goes, if we do not know where we are going, we will probably end up somewhere else.

One glance at our daily routine illustrates how consistently we react with our emotions and follow our emotional instincts instead of using thought-directed behavior. The mind, not the feeling, should direct our behavior. We often prefer reacting from our "gut" to acting through our heads.

From the locker rooms of every sport we hear coaches droning to their players, "Let's get out there and play harder!" However, what coaches really want is to have their teams play smarter. Reason and rational thought processes are much more effective in attaining victory than tired bodies, aching muscles, and fluctuating emotions. In competitive sports, a player needs to fuse all her muscles, emotions, and thinking process together to produce maximum effort. By playing smarter, we are not letting our emotions and tired muscles make the decisions. Instead, our thinking power must take charge. In our daily lives, as in competitive sports, we must allow our intellect to dictate our emotions and actions.

What I am again talking about is a balance of thought with feeling, individual rights with social responsibility, self with other. A study of the martial arts provides us with an example of this balance within one arena. Every action is undertaken with the knowledge of where one is, has been, and wishes to go. Every movement is made with the awareness of self and other and the consequences on both. One learns to be always aware, to use one's head rather than giving way to emotions, and yet to move with the flow of one's intuitions based on that mindful awareness.

☐ What Color Glasses Are We Wearing?

Cognition is defined as the process of knowing or perceiving. Our perceptions can have a significant impact on our lives. Drs. Aaron Beck and Albert Ellis, who pioneered the concept of Cognitive Therapy, focused attention on cognitive distortion as the root of unhappiness and mental illnesses. Like Confucius, both Beck and Ellis feel that it is not what we see, but how we perceive it that will color our responses and influence our actions.

Our minds can control, direct, and intervene in our body's physiological or emotional functions. In addition, our minds can cause or cure disease, eliminate or induce distress, and fill us with sorrow or happiness. It follows, then, that it is the content or quality of our thoughts that is most significant in our daily lives. If we accept that cognition is the most important component in the human experience, then it would be immensely beneficial if we were to change our attitudes and beliefs by eschewing our biases, and prejudices and ridding ourselves of negative influences. Instead of trying harder to live by our old values and beliefs, we should live smarter by changing our attitudes and perceptions of society and the world around us.

Cognitive therapy teaches that we can attach any perception we wish to an event; thus, we can control and direct our feelings and actions. We can certainly program ourselves to think positively and to live by our thinking. We must believe that no matter how bad something is, something good will come out of it.

> Your mind will be like its habitual thoughts; for the soul becomes dyed with the color of its thoughts.
> —*Marcus Aurelius*

Many people might call these positive attitudes naive or idealistic, but positive attitudes enable us to handle life's events with flexibility and equanimity. In the end, we will live happier and more satisfying lives than those who insist on dwelling on the negatives. A positive attitude does not just occur naturally in most people. It is a conscious and deliberate decision making process. We all have a choice in the matter. Research indicates that optimism is vital to our health and quality of life, and may be more relevant to our achievement level than ability (Seligman, 1998). Do we want to look on the bright side of life's events or are we determined to be pessimistic and negative?

All thoughts and perceptions must first pass through our brains and be processed; then we react on the thoughts with emotion or action. Just as the larger world influences us, we are also affected by our relationships with members of our family, schools, and church. But personal life events and environmental influences, regardless of how painful or cruel, cannot affect our mental and physical equilibrium unless our mind first gives its consent. Our coping mechanisms—whether fluttering out of control, like a kite blown astray by a strong gust of wind, or being steadily guided toward the future—will determine the way we perceive and interpret life's events.

Our emotions, judgments, and behavior result from our cognitive process; if our thinking is distorted and we are internally programmed to view life negatively, then our lives will invariably be filled with unhappiness, regret, and pain.

Our personal happiness is directly related to our perception of life's events and the people around us. Many of those in the field of cognitive therapy believe that most unhappiness is not caused by misfortune or the unpleasant aspects of real life events, but rather by distorted perceptions of reality. The old cliché about looking at life through rose-colored glasses is actually good and practical advice: our tainted vision can be corrected by looking through rose-colored lenses to re-orient and balance our interpretation of life's events.

Dale Carnegie wrote many books about the power of positive thinking, and I agree wholeheartedly with his vision (see Carnegie, 1936). We can best help ourselves by making a deliberate and conscious effort to remain positive and understand that we always have personal choices that are ours alone. After all, human emotions are the product of our perceptions that we can choose, direct, and control.

☐ Lives of Fantasy and Illusion

Those who cannot see through cognitive distortion or biased interpretation will assign great value to efficiency, rationality, and perfection. For these people, life can only be filled with frustration and unreachable goals because by refusing to acknowledge that there are human limitations, they continue to pursue a course that is contrary to human reality. They put heavy pressure on themselves and others to strive for unrealistic and unattainable goals and then experience failure, guilt, and self-abasement when they discover that they cannot reach them.

In a world of limits, it is not possible to expect perpetual and constant perfection. Such an irrational expectation of self or of others is inconsistent with reality and human nature. It is automatically programmed to fail. If we build our lives with illusion and fantasy, we will not be able to accept or understand misfortune, mistakes, or failure. Thus, life will be a big disappointment for us. We will rarely be happy because any achievement short of being "number one" will be unacceptable. With such expectations, it will be virtually impossible to have satisfactory human relationships.

☐ Biases Are Based on Distorted Reality

Most racial, cultural, and sexual discrimination arises primarily from a distortion of reality. This distortion comes from valuing the self over and above esteem for others. Irrational perceptions and culturally biased negative attitudes distort reality. Preconceived ideas prevent us from having a clear vision of reality. Broad generalization about others—especially harsh, negative stereotypes—breed fear, hatred, and discrimination. From children on a playground making silly faces at someone they perceive to be different, to the subtle prejudices instilled by parents and society, we have imprinted and fostered the beginning of social discrimination and irrational hatred. We can project the consequences of these influences to future street gangs, racial hatred, and ethnic warfare. In short, other-esteem is totally absent.

Each one of us must acquire a higher level of tolerance for the differences in others. We must increase our personal willingness to listen and to accept all members of the human family. Searching for the traits we have in common is certainly more productive than criticizing ethnic or cultural differences. Far too often, we have focused on cultural differences and personal preferences, while ignoring common aspirations and spirits of give-and-take. We are in this world together and there is enough room for all of us.

Technological advances in telecommunications have electronically shrunk our universe. A sneeze heard in China can receive a reply of "gesundheit" from Germany, "bless you" from North America, and "salud" from Mexico—all within seconds of the first "achoo." These advances have drawn our world's nations closer together, hopefully for the better.

With the world shrinking so rapidly, it is time for us to take a hard look at our distorted biases and begin to teach and encourage tolerance and open-mindedness within ourselves, our children, and our societies. Our economies are increasingly interconnected, and interdependence among different countries is the wave of the future. We need to learn, understand, and practice the business ethics and protocols of different cultures. We must research their preferences and choices. Not everything American should be exported without modification. Nor can we assume that what is good for the United States is also valuable to the people of other countries.

☐ Our "Twisted" Minds

An example of the stress that mental distortions can cause is illustrated by the following narrative. You are flying to Denver to meet a special new friend. You have talked with her on the phone and know that she is planning to meet you at the airport. When you arrive at the airport, however, she is not there to meet you at the gate. How do you react? What thoughts go through your mind? Do you begin to think "She didn't like me that much after all . . . she has probably found someone else and didn't have the courage to tell me." "Maybe I should book the next flight home." Do you start worrying, thinking "Oh my God, I bet she had a terrible car accident. What if she is lying maimed in a ditch? How can I find her?" Or do you calmly move with the crowd to the baggage area, reasoning that she will meet you there because it is an easier place for her to find parking? The first two reactions are the stuff heart attacks are made of—depression, panic, and negativity. The third reaction shows less stress and more mature, clear thinking. The point is that there are many ways to let our thinking make matters worse—or better—for ourselves.

☐ From Bad Luck To Good Fortune

My parents related the following story to me when I was still a young child. In ancient China, there lived a hard-working and wealthy merchant who owned a large piece of farmland. All the tracts of his land were producing profitable crops every season except for a single large section in the southwest corner. Nothing would grow on this particular tract. He tried many different crops, using all the methods known at the time, yet still nothing grew. He simply could not understand why this land was so unprofitable.

The farmer began to ask advice from friends, associates, and well-known astrologers. He even consulted the "Fung Shi" experts. ("Fung Shi," literally translated means "wind and water." It was an ancient Chinese method of divination regarding the harmony of the elements of nature and their juxtaposition.) All the Fung Shi experts gave him the same advice: it is a sign of bad luck. He should sell the property and move somewhere else. Unwilling to accept failure, he rejected their advice.

One day, while watching his children playing in water puddles in the fields, the farmer had a startling idea. He immediately began to design a plan to turn the undesirable corner of his property into a huge Chinese garden with beautiful ponds filled with colorful fish and a variety of water lilies. When the expansive garden was finished, friends and neighbors in the village marveled at its beauty and serenity, and asked permission to visit the garden to enjoy its peacefulness. The garden drew so many visitors that the farmer began to charge admission. But still the crowds kept on coming. Soon he added a teahouse to serve tea, snacks and lunches. In less than one year, this new garden brought him more financial gain than any single tract with a full crop in any season. Bad luck? No indeed . . . good fortune!

Another similar story makes the point in another way. A Chinese farmer has a magnificent horse. One day his son leaves the gate to the corral open and the horse runs away. His neighbors say, "Oh, how unfortunate." He replies, "It is as it is." The next day, the horse returns leading a herd of beautiful wild horses. His neighbors say, "Oh how fortunate." He replies, "It is as it is." The next day, his son breaks his leg trying to ride one of the wild horses. His neighbors say, "Oh, how unfortunate." He replies, "It is as it is." The next day the army comes to conscript all the able-bodied men of the village to fight in a war. The son does not have to go because of his leg. The story goes on and on in this manner.

Both stories remind us that it is our attitudes and what we do with them that shape our responses to our lives. Sometimes there are things that happen that are beyond our control, and what may look like a tragedy may, in fact, be the seed for a garden of bounty. It is up to us to determine how we react and to make the most of life's ups as well as downs.

☐ Expanding Our Vision

We must not let ourselves become "victims" of our emotions. Once again, perception is very important. Nothing can affect our emotions or elicit certain behavior without our mind first processing the input. Emotion comes only after perceptions have been processed by our minds. Therefore, our mind has to decide and consent to our anger, irritation, joy, and happiness.

How often have we heard ourselves crying out loud in moments of frustration: "But I have no choice!" When we hear these words, we must immediately STOP. Take a deep breath, relax, and tap into our inner self and say: "I always have a choice!" The different choices or alternatives may not be readily apparent at first glance, but they are always there. Our family, intimate friends, and colleagues are often able to point the way to new directions and/or solutions that we are temporarily unable or unwilling to see. However, we alone must be the one to make the choices. We alone can dictate how we feel, how we think, and what we do.

☐ Giving Up Control of Our Lives

We are surrounded by people who continuously try to influence our actions, feelings, and way of thinking. In today's technological world where we are exposed to instant and extensive communication, it is extremely difficult to prevent such attempts at manipulation. Parents firmly coerce their children into certain preferred or acceptable hobbies or careers. Shrewd advertising blinds us to what a "successful" life should be. Persistent salespersons distort our perceptions of what we need and want. Our legal system assures us that we do not have to be held accountable for our mistakes and misfortunes; we simply need to sue someone else and make them pay. From every direction, we are constantly being bombarded by subtle forms of mind control, influence, and manipulation.

One of the most obvious signs of this problem in our society is the proliferation of weight reduction centers and diet control clinics in every city. Their existence implies that we are as a people we are blessed with too much of the good things in life, indulging in excesses, but with no idea what to do about it. It seems that most of us are living "the good life"—we do not exercise, and we eat and drink too much. We are amazingly creative at making up irrational excuses for our overindulgences. We have lost control of ourselves and have decided that we can no longer deal with our own health and physical well-being. Thus, we are willing to spend hundreds—even thousands— of dollars to let some supposed "experts" tell us what to do with our own bodies, our diets and health.

With thousands of diet centers doing a brisk business (making millionaires out of the promoters), we can only conclude that there must be millions of people willingly choosing to give up their self-directed-ness, handing over the control of their bodies instead to someone with the latest fad for weight loss. Many people careen from one weight reduction clinic to another, changing diet plans on a weekly or monthly basis, with the plaintive excuse, "The last one did not work for me."

Is the creative, successful solution to a weight problem going to be found in these centers, with their slick brochures and advertising for "guaranteed" techniques and methods? And do the pounds stay off once the program is over? For most people, the answer is a resound-ing "NO!" Research indicates that over 90 per-cent of the people who lose weight this way regain it within months of stopping the exter-nally controlled diet. They temporarily changed their eating habits, but not their lifestyle.

The secret to success in controlling our lives and habits is exactly what this book has been postulating all along. The answers do not lie outside—in diet centers or in gratuitous advice from friends, neigh-bors, peers, and strangers. We need one another for support, for en-couragement, and for the interdependence of ideas for growth and development, and we must all empower ourselves to find answers to our life's problems. The manipulative answers and solutions in which we are told what to do and how to think without using the ethical and moral values of self and society will lead to a continuation of the problems we see in our society now. By giving up our individual think-ing and values to merely do what we are told by others is morally bankrupt. But by using our inner moral compasses to interact in ways which are mutually beneficial, both self and other will gain.

The answers are within each one of us. If we begin with a will and desire to change, and gain the basic knowledge to adopt a sensible plan, we can then take control of our own lives. What needs to be changed is our lifestyle and outlook on life. These changes must be permanent, not temporary, short-term measures that we discard once our goals are reached. Once we attain our first

> To know what you prefer instead of humbly saying Amen to what the world tells you you ought to prefer, is to have kept your soul alive.
> —*Robert Louis Stevenson*

objective, we still need to maintain those goals and perhaps even set the next objective. Handing control of our minds and our bodies over to strangers will never be a permanent solution. A radical modification of our lifestyle, coming from the desire to change within us, is the most powerful tool.

☐ Three Fundamental Questions of Life

For centuries, Chinese sages have told us that in order for a person to attain joy and happiness in this life, that person must learn how to live a harmonious and balanced life of self, others, and nature. Once harmony is achieved with others, and with nature, a person will attain inner peace and tranquillity. It is a delicate balance of the three elements in our life that will produce this objective. One element cannot dominate the others, nor can one be allowed to eclipse the others. Each must have a high degree of regard and respect for one another. With this in mind, there are three fundamental questions that we can each answer to guide us to our road to happiness in life.

1. How can I learn more about my own strengths and weaknesses?
2. How can I acquire an understanding of and respect for others?
3. How can I maintain a harmony of self with nature?

☐ Easy Steps to Untainted Perception

The first step in seeing reality is to direct and challenge our "irrational beliefs," as Albert Ellis, founder of Rational Emotive Therapy, so aptly calls them. Our lives are filled with events and with people trying to impress their often selfish and biased opinions on our psyche. All day long, television soap operas, newspaper columnists, popular radio talk shows, etc., tell us how we should think, act, and feel. But what comes from the minds of others is not necessarily right. Such thoughts or suggestions may be harmful to us. In addition, we often bring with us into our adulthood irrational beliefs based on childhood perceptions of events we were unable to understand at the time. Most of us do not realize what a strong impact social environment has on us. John Bradshaw, host of the popular PBS television series and author of the book, *Bradshaw On: The Family*, emphasizes the importance of family in shaping our personalities and outlook on life. Our behavior with young children has a

> He who knows others is wise; he who knows himself is enlightened.
>
> —*Lao-Tzu*

profound effect on them as they grow into adults. The way we think, feel, and act will influence the kind of people they turn out to be.

We need to learn how to sift through all the different and varied stimuli coming at us from past or present events, to become more selective, and to be able to respond to them based on our chosen values and principles. Finally, we become aware of these avenues of mental manipulation or "brainwashing," acknowledge them for what they are, and identify the sources. If we can accomplish this, we will have taken the first step toward sorting out our own rational belief system from the beliefs that others are trying to force upon us.

The second step is to recognize that we alone have the power to select one perception over another. We alone can find the positive aspects of negative events, and focus on positive behavior rather than destructive actions. My years in counseling and consulting have shown me that many if not most people tend to focus more on the negatives than the positives. For instance, whether at home or in the office, we are often quick to assign blame when a mistake, accident, or error occurs. Instead of expending our limited time and energy in trying to assess who is responsible or accountable for the mistake, a more positive behavior would be to call everyone together, accept the fact that a mistake was made, and focus the time and energy on learning from the mistake. Turn the mistake into a learning experience. Ask and learn from our subordinates or children why the mistake happened and how it can be prevented from happening again in the future.

Trying to assess blame implies that we do not want to be held accountable for the mistake or error. How we handle such a situation reflects our perception of life's events. Do we dwell on the negatives and harp on something that has already occurred? Assessing blame will not make the error go away. Or do we decide to see the positives and turn the event into a learning opportunity for everyone? The first action is destructive, and the latter action is constructive and positive. We must truly believe that although our behavior is shaped and influenced by culture and society, we must decide personally how to approach life, and that is something that no one else can decide for us.

The third step is to learn how to share our thoughts with the people in our circle of support. (The circle of support will be discussed more fully in Chapter 4) Sharing our private thoughts with others is a vital reality check. All of us have a story to tell, usually a tale of how our lives turned into such a mess. In this case, others can give us a new perspective. On the other hand, we are sometimes not even aware that our lives are a mess, especially when our minds are blinded by emotional involvement, just as a person cannot see straight when drunk with alcohol. Believing in our own rights while emotionally drunk could lead to drastic catastrophic decisions. In the news, we hear of people every day who felt they had been wronged by others or life events and decided to take matters into their own hands. If we would only check out our thoughts with some trusted others, some of these tragic happenings might have been avoided. While friends don't let friends drive drunk, how can we allow our family members, colleagues, or friends to continue to live on as emotional drunkards?

> If friends don't let friends drive drunk, friends shouldn't let friends live in an emotional mess.
> —*Phil Hwang*

Many American pop psychologists have told us that we can do whatever we want and we can do it alone. This philosophy caters very much to the rugged individualism of American culture, but ignores the fundamental principles of inter-dependency. We are who we are because of others in our life. We must learn to see the world from other perspectives. We must perceive and interpret life events with others whom we trust and respect. Our way may not be the only way. Our solution may not be the only solution or even the best solution.

Once we are aware of our own belief system and understand that we can control and direct our perception of life and the world, the fourth and final step is to act on our new convictions. This means that even though we may not always have control over life's events, we will always have control over our *reaction* to the events. In taking this last step in achieving an untainted vision of life, we should be ready to accept responsibility for our actions and deeds. Acting upon our new convictions is knowing that our behavior is a direct result of our ability to choose and decide what is right and beneficial to us.

☐ Change Only What You Can

Many psychologists agree that it is the interpretation or misinterpretation of events that affects us the most. One common misperception most of us have is unrealistic expectations regarding life events. There are two types of events in our lives: those we cannot change, and those we can change. Most psychologists would have us focus primarily on what we are able to control and change.

Some of the events we cannot change or control are the weather, the families we are born into, our ethnic origin, the passage of time, and death. Although we may not be able to control these aspects of our lives, this does not mean we should be resigned to a life devoid of happiness and hope. Rather, we must learn to recognize "unchangeable events" for what they are and work with and around them instead of against them.

But we can readily control and change almost every other aspect of our lives. By discovering from our life experiences what works for us and what does not, what we can change and what we cannot change, and knowing how we are going to use this information to our advantage, we can finally take charge of our lives and put ourselves back in the driver's seat.

> The light is not at the end of the tunnel. It is inside the tunnel and the switch is right next to you. Turn it on now!
> —*Phil Hwang*

The most powerful perception of all is the awareness that it is within our control to turn crises into opportunities, disadvantaged social environments into powerful motivations for achieving excellence, and seemingly fatal events into mere inconveniences.

☐ The Choice Is Ours

There are only two ways to perceive and interpret the events of life: the distorted view and the rational view (see Figure 2.1). If we choose the distorted view, we will be negative, depressed, and constantly blaming others and events of life for our unhappiness. On the other hand, if we select the approach to rationality, we will become positive, realistic, and willing to accept responsibility for our own actions (see Figure 2.2). We will also learn to accept failures and setbacks as challenges and opportunities for growth. Finally, though the ultimate choice is

> List of NEW Beliefs in life:
> 1. Unhappiness is my personal choice.
> 2. My irrational beliefs are based on my erroneous perceptions.
> 3. There is no rational reason why I should have Blue Monday or TGIF.
> 4. My emotions are the results of my own mental attitudes, which are within my control.
> —*Phil Hwang*

ours, we can still learn from ours and others' life experiences (see Figure 2.3). We will soon be on the road to attaining other-esteem.

The choice is ours and the choice is clear.

> Whether your intention is to hurt or to flatter, it will always be interpreted according to each person's private perception of themselves and your intention has very little consequence in their reality.
> —*Chin-Ning Chu (1992)*

Key Concepts in This Chapter

1. Perception is everything.
2. Learn to interpret life events with others.
3. Cognitive distortions color your judgment.
4. Challenge your irrational beliefs and biases.
5. Change is within your reach.

---

1. *Today must not be my day!* This is a justification for your sloppiness, mistakes, and failures. You convinced yourself and informed others that you will not be responsible for anything today. You expect everything to go wrong. Of course, you are not responsible, since it is not your day. Since this is not your day, would you please go home and spare others of your misery? When you come to work tomorrow, make sure that it is your day.

2. *That's the last straw!* This statement sounds as if you have been collecting straws at every turn you make. They are all heaped on your back so that you are ready for the proverbial last straw that breaks the camel's back. In reality, it is another rationalization for you to get angry at someone and to let go of some steam. Stop collecting straws at every turn. Let each straw roll off your back immediately. Thus, the last straw will become your first straw always. There will be no reason to let go of your anger.

3. *I am not guilty!* This statement is so prevalent today that it seems irrational to expect otherwise. Rarely will you see someone step up and honestly say, "I did it!" Guilt or innocence is often based on individual rationalization of human actions and their consequences. Social mores used to command certain adherence and interpretation of right and wrong. Today, guilt or innocence is more often an individual choice and a legal manipulation by the legal system. This often shows a fear of consequences rather than a statement of truth or reality.

4. *Mondays are always bad days!* I can never understand why Monday should be a Blue Monday and that you thank God when it is Friday. Why can't you have a blue Friday and thank God for Monday? TGIM? Do you

really hate work that much? When you believe that Monday is "blue," you will not be happy on Mondays. This of course will affect your performance at work. When you start the day with the attitude that it is going to be bad, it very often becomes a self-fulfilling prophecy.

5. *I have no choice!* This simple phrase is often used by someone who does not want to take responsibility. You always have a choice, unless someone points a gun to your head or you are locked up in prison. A choice, however, may be limited and not to your liking. The freedom to choose also comes with responsibility to self and to others.

6. *Everybody is doing it!* This was a phrase echoed many times by looters during the Los Angeles riot of 1992. Since other people are doing it, it must be okay for me too. This is a generalization, not based on facts. You are not everybody. What do you want to do? The choice and responsibility are yours! During the recent earthquake in Kobe Japan, it was reported that there was not a single incident of looting. Nobody is doing it and therefore it is not OK?

7. *It is not my fault!* Do not blame your problems on a poverty-stricken childhood or abusive parents. Others may have had the same or similar circumstances and used them as a springboard to good. Fault-finding will not get you anywhere in life. Taking personal responsibility is the key to solving life's problems.

8. *Life is not fair!* Fairness in life is neither a birthright nor an attainable goal. People who constantly blame events and circumstances of life for their problems will never be happy or become effective individuals.

9. *He ruined my day!* Do not rely on others to give you happiness in life. Nobody can make or ruin your day unless you let it happen. You can make your own day, every day! Today you did it! Tomorrow you can do it! The day after tomorrow you can do it again!

10. *It is my right!* Others may have the same rights at the same time and may be demanding their rights at the same time you are so loudly demanding yours. If you are constantly aware of your responsibilities, perhaps you would not be as demanding of your rights. In addition, sometimes the things some of us call rights are actually not rights at all but privileges that may or may not have to be earned.

11. *I didn't mean to!* This is an excuse often given by one person who just hurt another. Maybe that person truly did not intend to harm anyone. However, intention is an invisible intellectual process, not an overt human behavior. People are hurt by how we act and not by our intentions. Perception is everything. Good intention is not enough. First, be aware of your intentions and behaviors before acting out. If those actions hurt another, be willing to accept responsibility, make amends, and do what is necessary to right a wrong.

FIGURE 2.1. Common irrational beliefs (excuses).

IRRATIONAL BELIEFS: List your own irrational beliefs.
(E.g., I can't do anything about my job.)

1. _____

2. _____

3. _____

NEW PERCEPTIONS: Show how you can refute them.
(E.g., I can get a better job if I get more education and learn new skills.)

1. _____

2. _____

3. _____

FIGURE 2.2. Irrational beliefs vs. new perceptions.

Circle the number on right that most closely describes your present attitude, feelings, or behavior. Indicate level of irritations experienced.

	1 = None	2 = Some	3 = Great Deal	4 = Extreme
1. People who call you "Honey" or "Baby."	1	2	3	4
2. Computer-generated telephone sales call.	1	2	3	4
3. Unable to find a parking space at the airport, prior to departure.	1	2	3	4
4. Beepers going off in churches, theaters, and concerts.	1	2	3	4
5. One who brags about personal achievements.	1	2	3	4
6. Drivers who cut in front of your car before freeway exit.	1	2	3	4
7. Served regular drink when you ordered diet or caffeine-free drink.	1	2	3	4
8. People who show up late, smile and do not even apologize.	1	2	3	4
9. Doctors, lawyers, etc. who do not see you at the appointed time.	1	2	3	4
10. Dining with someone using a 2-for-1 coupon, ask that you pay for the dinner and he/she uses the coupon.	1	2	3	4
11. Car alarms going off in the middle of the night.	1	2	3	4
12. Long lines in grocery, banks, airports, ball games, concerts.	1	2	3	4
13. People who lie to get what they want.	1	2	3	4
14. People who are nosy about your personal affairs.	1	2	3	4

FIGURE 2.3. Irritations of life.

The Conspiracy of Silence

"The cruelest lies are often told in silence."
—Robert Louis Stevenson

The woman slumped on our family room couch, tears streaming down her cheeks and sobs punctuating her words. As a long-time family friend, she had sought my advice regarding her fractured relationship with her 30-year-old daughter who had broken off all contact. "Not even a card on Christmas," the mother sobbed. "I'm no longer allowed to see or speak to my grandchildren! This is a high price to pay for something I didn't do."

The relationship collapsed recently when the daughter discovered, twenty years after the fact, that her mother had known of her husband's lengthy and repeated sexual abuse of the daughter. The mother had not done anything to stop the cruel and destructive behavior. The daughter now raged at her mother for not speaking out, for not seeking help, for not trying to protect her. She heaped the blame and responsibility solely onto the mother for her own mental agonies and sexual dysfunction. "If only you had spoken out and condemned his behavior, this would not have happened!" These were the final words my friend heard from her daughter.

Today the mother agonizes over her past mistakes and wishes desperately to explain to her daughter that she, too, was terrified of this abusive man and was "only trying to keep the family together." I said to her, "What family? You didn't have a family! In reality, by not speaking out against your husband's sexual abuse, you became a

43

co-conspirator." Not only did the mother not show feelings or esteem for her daughter, her silence and her lack of action showed total disregard for her daughter and what her daughter felt and went through.

☐ Deaf to Others' Silent Cries

This example illustrates one of the greatest tragedies of our society: it thrives on secrecy. Financial secrets, legal confidentiality, and religious privacy are common behaviors of our society. We keep quiet because we believe it is better for the person sharing the secret with us and we do not want to betray a trusting relationship (see Figure 3.1). We also think that without this secrecy, nobody will confide to us any personal or confidential information. Are all of these statements rational? We need to challenge and question some of these secrets some of the time. Keeping secrets from someone raises suspicions and suggests that something may be amiss.

We have all read and heard about instances of abusive relationships turned even more tragic as the abuse was allowed to escalate because no one stepped in. Often family members and friends knew of the

---

For which of the following social norms of "secrecy" do you believe are positive, helpful, and should be maintained?

1. Psychologist and client relationship.	YES	NO
2. Lawyer and client confidentiality.	YES	NO
3. Doctor and patient relationship.	YES	NO
4. Personal and business dealings of politicians.	YES	NO
5. Incidents of domestic violence and abuses.	YES	NO
6. Churches and pastoral relationships.	YES	NO
7. Gangs and teenage mischief.	YES	NO
8. Personal lives of the famous, rich, and powerful.	YES	NO
9. Unethical behavior of business colleagues.	YES	NO
10. Personal and intimate relationships.	YES	NO
11. Illegal activities of fellow students.	YES	NO
12. The boss' misuse of company resources.	YES	NO

FIGURE 3.1. Life's conspiracies of silence.

circumstances but kept quiet for fear of betraying confidences. Our silence and lack of action in the face of any abuse are inexcusable. It shows lack of other-esteem for the victim and perpetrator alike and is akin to letting an emotionally drunk person drive through life.

Upon hearing of such incidents, we are quick to condemn others for their lack of action and ask: "How could anyone let such cruel things happen right in front of their eyes?" Failure to act or speak out is unacceptable, especially when the actions of others are clearly wrong and will have tragic and fatal consequences if they persist. Our own excuses, vague words, and feeble rationalizations cannot compensate for a life lost or permanently scarred.

But as a society, we continue to ignore the screams for help and the pain and suffering. Instead, we hide behind the foolish rationalizations that if we ignore a problem, it will somehow eventually go away, or it isn't our business, or we shouldn't interfere, or we can't betray a trust, or (like my friend) it would break up the family. These rationalizations allow some to turn a deaf ear to their friends or even to their own children, whom they are supposed to love and nurture. This senseless silence has allowed the maiming and crippling of countless numbers of people. By shrugging off our responsibility to speak out or intervene, we not only give consent to the perpetrators, but actually condone such cruelties. In essence, we become co-conspirators and partners in the crime. No wonder abused children grow up to rage against a parent's broken trust.

☐ Confidentiality: The Glitter and the Tarnish

Confidentiality is well thought of by society. Those we consider our closest friends are the ones who can keep our secrets. In many industries and professions, confidentiality is a requirement. A certain degree of confidentiality in selected relationships is necessary and beneficial and is certainly firmly rooted in our society. For many centuries, Catholics have faithfully attended confession, knowing the priests listening to their dark secrets have taken a vow of absolute secrecy. Few would confess their sins to a priest if their confessions were not kept secret. In addition to the realm of religion, confidentiality is also practiced in many professions—namely with attorneys, doctors, and therapists. The legal profession can only function with privileged information. Investigative works and political negotiations at times demand secrecy until completion. However, in some instances, confidentiality contributes to the conspiracy of silence and can have a negative impact on both people and the environment.

☐ Secrecy Reinforces Negative Behaviors

The keeping of dark secrets and the swearing not to reveal information can work as a negative psychological reinforcer rather than as a deterrent to misbehavior. In other words, anything kept secret tends to perpetuate the continuance of the behavior or misbehavior. An absolute guarantee of secrecy or confidentiality without challenge and demand for change may not only reinforce negative behaviors, but also lessen the guilt of a transgressor and, in fact, foster an environment where people do not feel accountable or responsible for their actions.

> Price of Secrecy:
> Secrecy reinforces negative behaviors of the perpetrators.
>
> Each one of us have the responsibility to break the code of silence.
> —*Phil Hwang*

Once the guilt is temporarily relieved, with little or no admonition, old patterns of behavior can be continued with less guilt. Knowing that the person confided in will not divulge a perpetrator's misdeeds lessens the person's sense of guilt and encourages the possibility of repeated offenses. Past successes beget more risks and bolder actions in the future if justice is not served. Stealing a trinket successfully in a department store may eventually escalate to the theft of thousands of dollars in clothing. As many criminals have been quoted, "The first crime is the toughest. From then on, it's a piece of cake." Indeed, there is a sense of omnipotence that one feels when one commits a crime with impunity; thus the silence of others is no deterrence at all and can actually encourage more of the same misdeeds. Very few human behaviors will change when kept in secret or shared only to those sworn to secrecy. People change when their secrets are out in the open.

Put aside considerations of moral and legal issues regarding confidentiality and focus mainly on the concerns of mental health and normal healthy relationships. Is absolute confidentiality vital to the therapeutic process? Or is confidentiality helpful to the patient? Should confidentiality extend to cover all illegal, immoral, or unethical behavior when a person's well-being is at stake? Under certain circumstances confidentiality may be inappropriate and can be detrimental to individuals and society alike.

This is also true in the context of psychological therapy, especially if the therapist is a good listener or a warm, caring person as in the renowned tradition of Dr. Carl Rogers, famous humanist, who founded the person-centered therapy in the 1950s. Counselors trained in his belief system are taught to accept the person with "unconditional positive regard." In other words, the person is made to feel better.

But is this diminishing of guilt and simultaneous feeling better about the self healthy for the individual person? Most mental health workers respond positively; I take exception. I think it is shortsighted to focus only on whether a client or patient feels better now. In the long run, if there is no attitude or behavioral change on the part of the perpetrator, then his deviant or negative behavior will continue and may end up being a threat to himself or to others.

While feeling better is good and even necessary for an individual, the need for a change in attitude and behavior is vital. The confidante or therapist needs not only to focus on making an individual feel better about himself, but also on the consequences of the client's behavior. What is needed is to constructively challenge attitudes and behaviors that deviate too much from the healthy norm or that are potentially destructive to the individual and/or society.

The prevalence of confidentiality and silence in American society work against the principles of accountability and responsibility. People seem to believe that unless they are caught and proven guilty, they have no responsibility. We see it all around us: gangs often vandalize other neighborhoods but seldom their own. Drivers run stop signs and red lights when they are confident that there are no officers around. In a civilized society with law and order, citizens have to be accountable and responsible for their actions in order to co-exist peacefully together. This means being willing and able to accept the consequences and punishment for being a menace or threat to society. The fear of being caught and brought to justice is what deters people from committing crimes. Without the principles of swift accountability and responsibility, it is difficult for justice to be served. The conspiracy of silence and prevalence of confidentiality enables people to feel less accountable or responsible for their own actions.

☐ Breaking the Myth of Silence

Silence is often considered a virtue, an admirable personality trait. The conspiracy of silence starts at a very young age. We encourage this in young children when we tell them not be a "tattle-tale." By the time children start grade school, they already believe that snitching to authorities is worse than keeping quiet about what they see—from the bully stealing lunches to the stoner selling drugs. Children learn very quickly that society ostracizes those who are whistle-blowers.

This encouraged silence continues throughout our lives. In the work-place, we remain silent as colleagues cut corners on projects or skim funds from public or company accounts. In our private lives, in the name of honoring privacy and minding our own business, we react to domestic violence and rape with silence and embarrass-ment. Some powerful poli-ticians and noted church leaders have been able to prolong their indiscre-tions and abuses because those close to them kept quiet for fear of losing their jobs or giving up the benefits of working for such a power-ful and influential person. These examples are but a few we know about, but they certainly redefine the meaning of the word "co-conspirator."

> We are who we are because of others in our life. They influence us just as we affect them.
>
> —*Phil Hwang*

As we were growing up, we often prided ourselves on our ability to keep secrets. We learned it from parents who, no doubt, also believed in its virtue. But a strong value system and moral code must be in-stilled in children by mature and concerned parents, relatives, and teachers who understand that silence in the face of harmful behavior can be tragic and must not be tolerated. Children need to be taught, educated, and guided to be active participants with strong moral voices and actions.

True caring, friendship, and love, the foundations of life's happiness, are not based on the keeping of life's dark secrets but on showing other-esteem by being an active voice in the lives of those around them.

☐ Speak out Now

The obligation of friendship demands sincere caring, even when it hurts. To merely listen but not to honestly say how you feel about a friend's actions is an example of a superficial relationship. Speaking out does not mean gossiping. Nor does it mean carelessly telling all your friends about what was said in secrecy. But if the behavior is harmful to yourself and others, the course of other-esteem demands your immediate action.

As a friend, it is your responsibility not only to voice concern but to inform the proper authorities if necessary. Suppose a friend confides that he is having an affair with a married woman. Do you pretend that you do not know or understand? What would you do if you discover that a friend is addicted to drugs? Do you pretend not to notice? A friend is aware of her husband's sexual molestation of their children, yet she does nothing. How can you ignore the terrible trauma that hurts young children when you know that both their parents are in collusion to harm the kids? Clearly these are difficult situations in which your involvement will most likely create problems and embarrassment for everyone. Yet the price of your silence and inaction is the continuation of horror and pain.

Speaking out is by no means an easy task. It takes great courage and strength to challenge irrational beliefs and behaviors. It is also not easy to risk losing the friendship and regard of those you love and care about when you do speak out. Those whom you are trying to help may not appreciate your intervention and, in fact, may resent your involvement.

One important thing to remember is that by speaking honestly, you are not imposing your values on others. You are challenging and questioning their actions and behavior but, regardless of what you say or do, the ultimate choice to listen, reconsider, and act is still theirs to make.

Having the courage to break the conspiracy of silence means condemning the actions and behavior, not the person. Our affluent society is suffering from a wide range of social ills because few of us seem to care enough or have courage enough to speak out about our convictions. Why are we so reluctant to speak out openly about what is right and wrong? There is too often a bewildering silence, especially when it comes to the rights of abused children, battered women, and innocent victims. We seem to have our priorities mixed up. We need to be aware of the long term consequences of our silence. Offending someone is far less serious, for example, than allowing a child to be hurt.

When we care enough to speak out, our actions can have a significant impact on those around us. It can, in some cases, mean the difference between life and death. The bumper sticker expression, "Friends don't let friends drive drunk," takes on a broader and deeper meaning in this context. Friends also should not allow friends to perform dehumanizing, brutal, or abusive acts that will have tragic consequences on the self or others. Speak out now.

☐ Why We Become Unwilling Co-Conspirators

There are at least five reasons why we become co-conspirators:

1. We are unwilling to lose, confront, or hurt a friend.
2. We are programmed early in life to be independent and individualistic and to mind our own business.

3. We fear reprisals from individuals or groups affected.
4. Society lacks a strong set of moral codes of ethics/principles.
5. We enjoy the power and excitement as a keeper of a dark secret.

☐ The Courage to Speak Out

Speaking out takes courage. It means taking risks. Other-esteem demands that we overcome our fears for self by speaking out and acting with others' welfare in mind.

The most common excuse for keeping a secret is the belief that divulging information would demonstrate a failed trust. We do not want to risk losing the trust of a friend or loved one. We feel that if we do speak out, this person may not confide in us anymore; worse still, he may be so angered by our thoughts, advice, or intervention that we become persona non grata to them, perhaps forever. But when a friend is harming himself or others, courage must take precedence over fear.

As discussed in Chapter One, embedded within American society is the belief that independence and individualism are virtues. Therefore, most of us grew up believing that it is virtuous to mind our own business. We developed an attitude of "I do not care what is happening around me, as long as it does not affect me. I do not want to become involved." In our society, there is pride in being different from everyone else, in being mavericks, and in standing out from all others. Furthermore there is a high value placed in the right to privacy and a fear that, by invading the privacy of others, our own coveted privacy may be lost. It takes courage to go against these social expectations.

The attitude of minding our own business permeates social institutions as well. In the past, teachers and school officials have been very reluctant to be involved in the personal aspects of their students' lives, even when sexual or physical abuse was suspected or even evident. Adults did not listen to or believe children who said they were molested or physically abused. Although it is now legally mandated that suspected abuse be reported by teachers, counselors, etc., law enforcement organizations have not adequately addressed this issue and others, such as spousal domestic violence. In some cases, children and women were maimed or died because officials felt it was not their responsibility to become involved in domestic squabbles.

Our unwillingness to speak out and become involved has covered up scandals and illegal and unethical behavior by individuals and organizations. Corporate and government corruption, reports of police brutality, and evidence of sexual offenses within the church hierarchy—

from the ranks of the Catholic clergy to Jim Bakker's exploits with the PTL—have been uncovered in recent years, but our silence allowed these offenses to continue unimpeded; thousands upon thousands of people have suffered as a result. There is no justice in silence, for justice cannot be served until the silence is broken.

Social pressure also works against speaking out and breaking the conspiracy. Those who speak out risk being resented and derided by people who resent having the status quo disturbed, their lives interrupted, or the need to change, even if it is for their own good. People with the courage and conviction to speak out are often not well thought of by society; they are often called whistle-blowers, informers, busybodies, snitches, tattletales, or gossipmongers—not very flattering or positive descriptions, to say the least. But speaking out means having the courage to risk reprisals and social pressures.

In some cases, there is fear of not just losing friends or incurring social displeasure, but fear that breaking the conspiracy of silence may result in financial harm, such as losing a job or, worse yet, threats of or actual physical violence. The fear of reprisal starts young. Children fear speaking out against bullies, gang members, or drug dealers due to the threats of being hurt.

Sometimes, unfortunately, these fears are well based. A story aired on "60 Minutes" illustrated the complexities and consequences of not speaking out versus breaking the silence. The story described the plight of a young man who claimed that he was wrongly accused and convicted of murder and is now serving a life sentence. The story unfolded years ago, when the young man was a teenager. One evening, he was riding his bicycle home and witnessed two gang members shooting a security guard. The next day, the teenager was cornered by the same two gang members and threatened with bodily harm if he said anything. That same evening, as news of the murder was televised and police were mounting an investigation, the gangs' members came to the teenager's home and again threatened to kill him and his sisters if he ever told the police what he saw. Thus, the teenager kept his mouth shut. His silence enabled the two gang members to falsely testify against him to the police and in court. On the strength of the two gang members' testimony, the teenager was advised by his attorney to plead guilty, and was sentenced to life imprisonment. The story does not end here. After the young man broke his silence and the media picked up on his story, one of his sisters was murdered. Through fear, the young man kept his silence and as a result was convicted for murder; when he broke his silence, he lost his sister.

One might think he paid dearly for speaking out. However, one wonders what would have happened if he had spoken out in the first place. Indeed, he has had to pay a very high price for his silence. But had he spoken the truth about what he witnessed as well as the threats to himself and his family, steps could have been taken to punish the true perpetrators of the crime and to protect those threatened. More often, the results of speaking out are positive and not negative or nearly so dire. Social ills, personal crises, and even petty annoyances cannot be attended to or corrected until someone stops the conspiracy of silence that enables them to continue and allows us to redirect our thoughts and actions to a more positive course.

Another reason for our silence is that society has lost the strong moral code by which everyone once abided. We live in a very diverse culture that is becoming increasingly pluralistic. We are not a homogeneous society, and our sense of morality and ethics—of agreement on what is right and what is wrong, what is ethical and what is unethical, what is good and what is bad, and of what is moral and immoral—is not very clear. On this point, our society has given in to a more individual, subjective interpretation rather than a collective objective moral philosophy. If we were to survey a thousand people and ask each to state his moral philosophy, we would end up with hundreds of different answers. What one person thinks is wrong, another person may think is right, and vice versa.

We have become too situational and our logical reasoning too clouded with sentimental excuses. We have too many persons and circumstances to blame for our predicaments. More examples: a woman spilled a cup of coffee on her lap and burned herself. She blamed McDonald's for making their coffee too hot, sued, and won a judgment of $3 million. The Menendez brothers of Los Angeles shot and killed both their parents. They claimed early childhood emotional and sexual abuses as their defense. Separate trials resulted in hung juries. Have we become a society of victims blaming everyone and anything for our misfortunes and unwilling to take responsibility for our own behaviors? Have we become a group of inward-looking and outward-blaming people?

Some may ask, "What is wrong with people having different opinions?" After all, we are all entitled to our own views and are free to express them when we like. There is nothing wrong in having different opinions about many aspects of life; in fact, everyone should be encouraged to view life from different perspectives. However, when it comes to moral philosophy, it is a more complicated matter.

What is morality? According to Socrates, morality—in the most general sense—deals with the question "How ought we to live?" Every society needs a moral code in order that everyone can peacefully coexist. Chaos and anarchy ensue in societies and communities that do not agree on how Socrates' question ought to be answered. In almost all civilized societies, murder, stealing, and lying are all classified as wrong, immoral, illegal, or unethical. However, most societies have moral codes much more complex and detailed.

If we lack a strong conviction between right and wrong, is it any wonder that we remain silent? How can we speak out strongly if we are not

> Every time you don't follow your inner guidance, you feel a loss of energy, loss of power, a sense of spiritual deadness.
> —*Shakti Gawain*

quite sure that what is being done is wrong? When we are sure, there may be ten other people who would disagree. In the United States, there is a lack of a strong social consensus on what is right and what is wrong, and the traditional family—the primary vehicle for the transmittal of moral values—has broken down.

The sad state of our ethics and virtues is not a new development. Philosophers and social scientists have written quite extensively on this topic during the past few decades. Such works as *Reconstructing Public Philosophy* (1982) by William Sullivan, *The Elements of Moral Philosophy* (1986) by James Rachels, and *After Virtue* (1984) by Alasdir MacIntyre all deal with the lack of coherence in American moral philosophy. The chain of silence can only be broken if Americans are able to reach consensus and agree to abide by and enforce a strong moral tradition. It takes courage to stand up for one's values and ethics.

The fifth reason we do not speak out is that some people relish the perceived control, power, and excitement of being able to keep someone else's deep, dark secrets. We have a certain craving for the titillating and juicy stories of human relationships and want other people to tell us about their life's messes. There is a certain degree of self-satisfaction, smirkiness, and even contentment in knowing something that others do not know. We rationalize our silence by saying that since we were told in secrecy, we have no responsibility to do anything. Wrong! If the secret is destructive, we have the responsibility to speak up and intervene. It is courageous to give up perceived power and control to be other-oriented.

☐ Break the Silence: The Need to Speak Out

Society as a whole is changing ever so slowly, but I do believe the general population is losing patience with the silent and blind acceptance of our many social ills. People are beginning to wake up, as grizzly bears emerging from a long winter's hibernation, hungry to stop cruelties and craving to take a stand against unacceptable and detrimental human behavior. Neighborhoods are organizing patrols to re-claim the streets from drug pushers and dealers. Non-smokers now know the deadly results of second-hand smoke and are asserting their rights to clean air. "Safe" houses to shelter abused women and children are increasing in numbers, and traumatizing events happening behind the privacy of closed doors are slowly being forced into the healing sunlight.

The need to speak out is particularly important for those who are in influential positions or are respected by society. As role models for the populace, it is important for community leaders to set good examples. Nevertheless, our leaders are human beings and they are not perfect. Persons in power may lack moral conviction and strong will; they may refuse to act or change their minds in their commitments to sensitive issues. Many are afraid to voice their convictions because they fear being politically wrong. But they are only running away from their responsibilities.

What is the ideal model leader? One with strong convictions who is willing to stand up under pressure for her beliefs and values. An effective leader must have the courage to be wrong, to make mistakes, and to accept responsibility for them. Being a good leader is not a popularity contest, and being right does not necessarily mean being popular. There are many instances when a leader has to do things that are for the good of the people and community, but not everyone may like it or agree with his position. A good leader knows that it is almost impossible for everyone to be happy all the time but has the courage to speak out and act in accordance with other-esteem.

If friends don't let friends drive drunk, why do I let my friends go through life emotionally distressed?

For whom do I need to speak out and intervene today?

1. _____
2. _____
3. _____
4. _____
5. _____

FIGURE 3.2. Am I a co-conspirator in silence?

Who are the leaders in society? Being a leader, in a general sense, means being in a position to influence the thinking and behavior of others. Parents, teachers, an older sibling, a manager, a therapist, actors or actresses, politicians, doctors, lawyers, scout troop leaders, or newscasters, for example, are all in a position to influence others. Most of us, at one time or another, will occupy a position of leadership.

To prepare for this, we must examine our behavior and attitudes as role models for others. We must have the courage to speak out and stand up under pressure for our beliefs and let others know when our moral tenets are challenged. As leaders, not only must we personally speak out, we must also encourage others to do so. Together, with them, you can break the conspiracy of silence. This is a true sign of other-esteem.

☐ Key Concepts in This Chapter

1. Secrecy reinforces negative behaviors of the perpetrator.
2. Your silence makes you a co-conspirator (see Figure 3.2).
3. Other-esteem demands that you speak out.

4
CHAPTER

Discovering the Inner
Ring of Intimacy

"One can never win trust of others by trying to dominate them. One can
only succeed by caring for their welfare."

—Mencius

Our society urgently needs to promote other-esteem in personal intimacy and in family relationships. There is a great lack of respect,
acceptance, and esteem for each other in many aspects of human
intimacy. The needs and wants of the self influence more relationship
decisions than concerns for the feelings and consequences of others
affected. It is looking out after Number One at all costs and in all
circumstances.

Intimate relationships today portray a confused, scattered and con-
flicted picture of human togetherness. At one end of the spectrum,
there is the group of people who believe in the sanctity of marriage,
family values, and religious teachings. They support each other with
respect, care, esteem, and love. Their marriages usually endure, and
traditional values are very important in the rearing of their children.
Their lifestyles are rather simple and conservative, yet meaningful
and connected. They possess a built-in support system of relationships
with significant others at various levels.

At the other end of the spectrum, relationships are temporary, emotional, selfish, and individualistic. We are all extremely cognizant of
the high divorce rate in our society. In addition, there are many types
of temporary living arrangements, with just as many move-ins and move-
outs. Living together for this group sometimes seems like a short term-
use of one another's emotional support and temporary satisfaction of

57

mutual sexual or monetary needs. A person in this group can fall in and out of love within a short period of time and even be intimate with different people at the same time. Love to these people has become an excuse rather than a reason for intimacy.

This is a sad commentary on our present day society. If there are people who do not even practice other-esteem for those with whom they are intimate, how can we expect them to practice any some level of esteem for others outside of their intimate relationships?

Some of us make too many spur-of-the-moment decisions with respect to our individual emotional needs. We often do not consider the consequences of our emotionality. We fail to see the irreparable psychological harm inflicted on others by our actions. Where is our other-esteem?

☐ Myth and Fantasy About Love

Love is often the reason or fantasy of human relationships. It is likewise the camouflage or rationalization for getting out of one relationship and into another. During the early stages of any relationship, we enjoy each other's presence, and our partnership blossoms in the freshness of one another's company. At this stage we tend to ignore shortcomings and imperfections in the other person. We are blind with newfound love and such "details" are of no consequence. We may foolishly believe that our love will change and improve any quirks we may have noticed in our partners.

As time goes on, however, and we become more accustomed to the relationship, many of those human habits become annoying. Soon they become so glaringly offensive that we simply cannot tolerate them intruding into our daily life. Little annoyances like chewing food with one's mouth open, scuffing shoes on the floor, using incorrect grammar, or not wanting to help with certain chores soon become intolerable. "Dear Abby" reports that she receives stacks of mail from frustrated people whose partners commit the "unpardonable sin" of leaving the top off the toothpaste tube!

Obviously, our level of tolerance for others' shortcomings and limitations is very low. Unable to accept the little annoying habits of our partner, we become frustrated and angry. We let our intolerance blind our whole relationship. Soon, we begin to question the wisdom of having chosen this partner. Before long, many of us commence the process of dismantling our short-lived togetherness. We convince ourselves and our partner that we are no longer in love. By this time, we my convince ourselves that we love someone else.

One of the causes of such discord is the persistent myth and fantasy about romantic love. As we progress into the 21st century, there are still some school-age girls who read fairy tales and fantasize about a handsome young man who will sweep them away in a red convertible sports car to live happily ever after. No one tells these girls that Prince Charming may have bad breath, problems with alcohol, a mean temper, or no desire to work a day in his life. What a shock for them to find out that the man of their dreams is not perfect!

In our society, many boys grow up involved in sports, dreaming of space travel, or fantasizing about being a professional athlete. If they think about it at all, most of them figure that they will eventually marry someone like their mother who will look after their daily needs. It is quite a trauma for them to discover their spouse may not want to have children, may have a more successful career than they, and may prefer to travel on business trips by herself. Or that if they have children, she will also expect him to put in his fair share of caring for the baby, diapers and all.

☐ "Hello-Goodbye" Marriages and Divorces

I characterize many of our society's marriages as "hello-goodbye" relationships. At the first meeting (the hello) or encounter, friendship and attraction are immediate and emotionally spontaneous. The separation (or the good-bye) is just as quick and final. This kind of relationship is shallow and temporary. Las Vegas caters to this style of quick marriages and divorces. I learned recently about an "instant union" of a couple from Los Angeles. It took only seven days from the couple's first meeting at a friend's party to their jumping aboard a plane to get married in Las Vegas. How well do you think this couple knew each other before committing themselves? How long do you expect this "hello-good-bye" marriage to last? Maybe it was planned to be just a temporary marriage. Perhaps for some people, their perception of human intimacy has drastically changed to mere encounters between passers-by.

☐ Disposable Human Beings

How many of us are in this "hello-goodbye" mode of human relationship? Do we dispose of partners and close friends based on moods and feelings of the moment? We are a generation that has grown up in the midst of plenty. Our prosperity has made us take for granted our good fortune. Our lives revolve around the acquisition of material things, forever trapped in a cycle of consumerism, endlessly acquiring and discarding physical things. Do we possess this inexcusable negative attitude and self-centered behavior towards our possessions and carry them into other aspects of our lives? Have we begun to apply the same disposable mentality to our relationships with other human beings? Have we taken to acquiring and discarding friendships and relationships just like we do our cars, computers, and stereos?

Some of us treat family members and significant others as if they are disposable items with a temporary status. We consider them low priority and mostly disregard or neglect them until we have need of them. We think more of ourselves and plan for our own happiness; we do not care much for the spouse, except when it comes to splitting properties and custody of the children. Some of us discard children, spouses, and even elderly parents like last season's fashion trends. We do not worry enough about the consequences of our actions, nor do we consider the profound emotional effect our behavior has on those near and dear to us.

We are rapidly losing the permanent aspect of intimate human relationships so prevalent in our parents' and grandparents' generations. In past generations, the centrality of the institutions of marriage, church, and family held American society together. With such institutions going strong, relationships had both permanence and commitment. In today's society, commitment is a taboo word, to be avoided at all costs. Have we lost the meaning of intimate relationships?

Such bonds are not merely pieces of paper, rings, candle-lit church ceremonies, or physical attraction. Bonds represent years of shared joys and sorrows, growing older and presumably more intimate, raising children and offering the mutual support that can only come from a deep, caring respect and esteem for each other.

Researchers have found that married people live longer than single people and report a higher incidence of happiness and sense of well-being. Married people commit fewer crimes and are jailed less often than single adults. Why? Because human beings are born for each other. People who commit themselves to each other, sharing common goals and interests, seem to have more at stake, and thus have a tendency to become more responsible and caring. Increased happiness and well-being also encourage people to become more generous with their affections for others and to view life in a more positive light.

☐ Joys and Pains of Love

It is our unrealistic expectations of love, marriage and relationships that cause us so much trouble. Cognitive distortions prevent us from viewing love from a practical and realistic point of view. As youngsters, we were inundated with fairy tales, stories, movies, and books that romanticize and idealize love. Nowhere are we taught that love sometimes causes pain and suffering, means sacrifice, and is not always a "head-over-heels" feeling. We are unprepared to accept the reality that love does not make a person perfect. Just because we are in love, it does not mean that all our annoying little habits will simply disappear into thin air.

The pop psychology books of the 1980s produced a torrent of new theories about myths of romantic love. Many writers agree that myths and fantasies have generated unrealistic expectations and unfulfilled desires. We see only the beauty and smell only the sweet fragrance of the roses, and ignore the thorns surrounding the flowers and our inability to preserve their fragile beauty beyond a few days. Living together in a committed relationship, however, is a bumpy road of life, and it demands a realistic and balanced response to the varied ups and downs of human life events.

Are the myths of romantic love a main reason that the divorce rate in this country is so high? Which comes first, the mass media's portrayal of flimsy human relationships, or society's actual decay of marital integrity? It is crucial to understand that although it is physical attractions that bring human beings together, it is love and esteem for one another that endures.

There are some who go through this human dismantling process numerous times without appearing to be affected by it. They change partners as if they are following the fickle fashion trends. The old, outdated relationships are cast aside as soon as new and fresh ones come on the market.

Relationships are a very special and unique human experience, worthy of our energy and meant to be treasured. They are not, and can never be, likened to the simple principles of supply and demand. Of course, there is love, joy, and fulfillment, just as there will be conflict, sadness, and disappointment. That is the very definition of a relationship. But the true challenge of living together and loving each other is measured by the amount and degree of our personal esteem for each other. It is easy to say "I love you" on our wedding day, but will it be just as easy on our tenth anniversary? Our thirtieth anniversary? As one comedienne asked, "Sure you love me now, with my youth and beauty . . . but will you still love me when I have false teeth and blue hair?"

Many of us want relationships during the good times, but not during the bad. If we have already accepted the principle that certain life events are unfair, then it follows that we are realistic enough to realize that living in a committed relationship demands personal sacrifice and compromise.

Accepting this axiom from the beginning of a relationship means that when true sacrifices are demanded, we will be better prepared mentally to deal with events as they arise. It is to be hoped that this attitude will prevent our scurrying away from the problems and trying again somewhere else without having learned from the problems. This acceptance of your partnership "through thick and thin" can help eradicate personal fantasies that romantic love is all that is needed to live happily ever after.

☐ Love Alone Is Not Enough

In the sphere of intimate human relationships, we often hear the saying, "I am so-o-o in love!" or "Love is blind." Are these catchy phrases really irresponsible expressions that permit irrational emotions and behaviors to bubble to the surface? Are we using such phrases as a rationalization for unacceptable behavior? If love is truly blind and our emotions overwhelm our rationality, we will most likely end up suffering disappointment, pain, and regrets.

How many of us have learned this lesson too late? Throughout history, more wars, deaths, and human misery have been wrought due to people's emotional response to their supposed feelings of romantic love than from any other reason. Even our mythologies and literature mirror this as seen in the stories of Helen of Troy, Romeo and Juliet, and King Edward VIII of England. Reflect also on some of our own personal foolish love affairs. If we only knew . . . hindsight is always 20/20 vision.

The components of any successful relationship include a high degree of compatibility, openness, honesty, sharing of one's self, and a high degree of tolerance and acceptance of each other's idiosyncrasies. True love is other-directed, not self-seeking. It is a team effort, withstanding the up-and-down challenges of living together with another human being as two persons share in the building of their future together.

Blindness in love is not a physical predicament, but rather a chosen cognitive distortion by the individual to allow the "child" to come out and play rather than to call on the "adult" to make a logical and rational decision based on untainted vision. Love is an emotion much like a roller coaster ride, racing up to the heights and careening through the dips. When we are on top, nothing seems to matter except our love for each other. When we sink into the low spots, however, or are climb-

> Blindness in love is a chosen cognitive distortion.
> —Phil Hwang

ing laboriously up the next hill, we should have basic, fundamental reasons for our togetherness, or those rails will split open and our relationship will crash.

All Relationships Can Be Enriching Experiences

In the realm of human relationships, we all know how tempting it is to break off at the slightest sign of disagreement or conflict. At times, it seems much easier to walk out the door than it is to stay and endure any pain and suffering needed to repair the relationship. There are, indeed, times when ending a relationship is the right thing to do for all concerned.

1. I have several people with whom I share my personal and intimate feelings.	YES	NO
2. Others come to me for help/advice/counsel.	YES	NO
3. Presently, I am in an intimate relationship with someone.	YES	NO
4. I feel useful to and needed by people around me.	YES	NO
5. I enjoy quiet time with people I care for.	YES	NO
6. I am happy at my present stage of life.	YES	NO
7. My colleagues at work support me.	YES	NO
8. I have a strong supportive system of family and friends.	YES	NO
9. I enjoy traveling with others.	YES	NO
10. I enjoy parties, picnics, etc., with friends.	YES	NO

FIGURE 4.1. Checklist for personal relationships.

There are relationships from which we need to get out fast, such as those which are destructive or abusive. These are mistakes in our life that need to be admitted, cleared, and from which it is best to move on. But by learning from these experiences, we can prevent them from happening again (see Figure 4.1).

There are also instances when a relationship is beyond repair. From time to time, we can choose to evaluate our personal needs, desires, aspirations, and dreams so as to make plans for the future. Over the years, people change, grow apart, or develop entirely different interests, behaviors, or goals. The original basis for togetherness may have eroded to the point where it may be a move towards good mental and physical health for the couple to make the mutual decision to end a relationship. This decision should not be considered a failure, nor treated as such. If the relationship is viewed as an enriching experience, full of learning that prepared each partner to better deal with future close personal encounters, it may be best to take that learning and move on without bitterness.

☐ Change Starts from Within

If we are willing to challenge irrational attitudes and learn how to re-focus our perception, we need first to look into ourselves. Are we fully aware that decisions involving relationship problems require adaptation, compromise and change? Even with this awareness, we seldom look inside ourselves for such solutions. The first thought is to criticize the partner, pointing out all the seeming faults and apparent shortcomings. We insist that "If you want happiness with me, you must first change your personality and your behavior!" We go to great lengths to change the other person, only to find out that it is an impossible assignment.

It simply is not possible for us to change another human being. Any fixing or changing in a human relationship must start with the self. The only way to have an impact on someone's behavior is to alter our own attitudes and behavior first. The questions should be, "What am I doing to help repair this relationship? Am I willing to take responsibility for my own personal happiness and dissatisfaction?" Change can only come from within. Our relationships change as our perspectives change. We have much more control over our actions and thoughts

> Change can only come from within.
>
> —*Phil Hwang*

than we realized. When we are willing to accept the statement, "I alone can change my own life, and I alone am responsible for my own happiness or sadness," we will make positive changes in our personal encounters.

☐ Esteem, Not Competition

Sociologists inform us that a high percentage of marriages are competitive. Husbands and wives who have no other-esteem constantly try to prove to each other, and to their children, that they are "better" than the other. They battle to demonstrate they are smarter, more understanding with the children, better organized, or a better money manager. Instead of respecting the partner for special talents and abilities that each possesses, one tries to outshine the other. This unhealthy competitiveness leads to jealousy, discord, and often a breakup of the union.

Everybody would like their intimate relationships be a constant honeymoon. This, however, is not realistic. Remember the words of the wedding ceremony, "for better or for worse"? At the time, we irrationally think there will not be a "for worse." Most of us have not accepted the reality that life will not always be easy or happy. We would like to believe that we deserve happiness and that we should not have to work for it. However, nowhere is there a guarantee that all relationships and marriages will be successful. These days, many marriages seem to be for the worse. The divorce rate is higher than ever before, and we more often read and hear about domestic violence, personal injuries, abuse, and even murders within the family.

We should stop our obsession with instant solutions and take an

> Progress must be quite gradual, and in order to obtain such progress in public opinion and in the mores of the people, it is necessary for the personality to acquire influence and weight. This comes from a careful and constant work on one's own mental development.
> —*The I Ching*

important lesson from nature: there are no shortcuts. As discussed in Chapter One, it takes time to grow beautiful roses, just as it takes time to find solutions to serious problems. Nature does not hurry her world, and neither should we. The mental health and peace of mind we achieve from slowing down can go a long way towards shoring up our relationships and marriages.

☐ Plan for Tomorrow's Togetherness Today

Social Security has many positive benefits, but it also fosters a negative climate. It takes away individual responsibility and the need for family togetherness and support. It is so easy to let someone else take care of us, but when that someone is the huge, impersonal, and bureaucratic government, we lose the ability to take charge of our own future. The importance of thinking and planning for tomorrow involves not only financial matters but also the more critical aspects of our lives—human relationships.

There are so many lonely, retired people in our country. Some of them seem to have been sent to institutions to await their final days alone, either because the relatives were unwilling to take the responsibility for care giving or unable to shoulder the financial or emotional burden.

But some of these individuals have a different problem. They are alone because in all their productive years they were never able to establish any significant human relationships. Their dealings with family and friends were shallow or antagonistic and bitter, and as they grew older, their ring of significant others gradually shrank into non-existence. They are often alone without understanding how the situation developed.

The importance of established and nurturing human relationships is critical to our mental health and should begin at a young age. Accepting others as they are, without a framework of myth and fantasy and unrealistic expectations, will not only make our youth and middle years more productive and exciting, but will enrich our later years as well.

☐ Togetherness Is First a Frame of Mind

With such a pervasive, transient, and almost universal attitude toward life, why are we perplexed by the resulting painful conflicts? Are we surprised by the breaking of the sacred bonds of intimate relationships, or that pre-nuptial contracts and agreements are becoming so common? People are already talking about divorce even before they get married! A temporary frame of mind cannot possibly make a positive contribution to the concept of stability and togetherness.

Unlike us, our parents grew up in the midst of war and poverty. The two world wars instilled in our parents an appreciation for stability and commitment, and the Great Depression taught them to save and conserve. During the toughest times, our parents' generation learned that it is often friendships and relationships that count the most and make life meaningful. Our parents lived in a "fix it" frame of mind. They repaired everything, from radios to plumbing to clothes and toys. They cared for automobiles so that they would last for decades instead of just a few short years. They also worked harder at "fixing" their marriages. It seems that during our parents' generation, there was a greater degree of tolerance for each other's shortcomings and idiosyncrasies. The "throw away" attitude that is prevalent now is a relatively new development. Previous generations of Americans simply did not needlessly discard objects or friendships or relationships.

Now we have a generation of baby boomers with a different set of priorities. As a group, they tend to be more self-obsessed and rebellious, and less committed to long-term relationships. They do not want to be tied down to just one person. They seem to embrace the "throw away" concept more than the "fix it." They often find it easier to run away from relationships than to repair them.

In the move away from commitment and stability in relationships, we have lost one of life's most important lessons: there is great satisfaction and reward in resolving conflict and friction. There is a beauty and deep-down satisfaction that comes with the realization that one has recognized the need for improvement and taken the necessary steps to fix a troubled relationship.

How do we fix troubled relationships? By showing a willingness to listen, discuss, negotiate, and compromise. It is through admitting that we do make mistakes and learning from them that we learn, improve, and gain in wisdom. I have yet to meet a wise person who does not listen to others and admit to imperfection. Fixing relationships forges stronger bonds and enriches human relationships. Such results are surely worth the efforts of a little more tolerance, patience, and humility on our part!

In Chapter One, we discussed other-esteem and the importance of relationships to the development of our self-identity and the whole of your life. However, if we cannot maintain our relationships, how can we lead a happy and satisfying life? If we were to always run away from relationships whenever conflict arises instead of staying and working it out, how could we learn where we went wrong? Without this knowledge, how could we change and improve? Those who avoid commitment and conflict in relationships are unlikely ever to reach emotional maturity or gain wisdom. Because there is so much mutuality in our relationships, we must realize that if we want others to trust us and accept us for who we are, we must be willing to do the same for them.

Intimate relationships also involve both nuclear and extended family members. Our parents, just like our offspring, are all pre-determined accidents of life. Our acceptance of this relationship for either group is absolutely unconditional. In other words, we have no choice on the selection of our parents, just as we have no choice on the selection of our descendants.

In contrast, we have absolute control over the choice of our intimate partner in life. Esteem for someone of our choosing is often easier than for those whom we inherited. But this esteem for our partner is also unconditional in terms of love, fidelity, compatibility, and more.

☐ Teaching Other-Esteem to Our Children

With our unconditional acceptance of our offspring comes the obligation and responsibility of teaching them other-esteem. We must provide life experiences and learning experiences so that they may acquire the principles and experiences of other-esteem early in life. Children in modern society acquire concept of self and other while still young. They enjoy so many modern conveniences that promote isolation and individuality rather than cooperation and interdependency. Many youngsters own a Walkman radio, with which they can tune out anyone anytime they choose. Some have their own room, phone, or television. These kids do not have to share, and thus they have no need to learn negotiation or the necessity of give and take in life.

A different way of looking at life in this situation is the practice of deprivation and delayed gratification. It is a great learning experience for children to give up certain things in life, even though we may be able to afford them. Teach children how to negotiate time on the family phone. Provide occasions for them to learn the needs of others. They may want to watch different programs on the television. Do not give in to their requests for instant gratification. Child rearing books instruct us to develop early the independence of your children. Although independence and self-sufficiency are desirable life-long traits and skills, they can become weaknesses and liabilities. Children can become independent so early that they do not understand the value of interdependency. Self-sufficiency is possible and valuable only up to a point. Beyond this, everyone needs someone to complete the wheel of meaningful life.

☐ Circles of Support

There is no doubt that we need each other. A healthier, happier, and more meaningful life-style demands that we deliberately and system-atically develop a net-work of support. Social support and intimacy may be the single most important factors in our mental and physical health (Ornish, 1998). Our basic

> Society promotes portable roots. We need to spend time, effort and even resources to develop our own ring of intimacy.
> —*Phil Hwang*

human need is to belong. We need to surround ourselves with people who genuinely care for and support us, just as we would do the same for them. Many of us have people around us who can be separated into two groups. I call these groups "Circles of Support."

The first (inner) ring is called the Ring of Intimacy (see Figure 4.2). It normally comprises six to eight very special and intimate persons. In some ways, this relationship is more sublime than spousal intimacy.

A. Identify your personal support system by listing as many people as possible in your Ring of Intimacy. (If you are unable to fill the above Ring of Intimacy, work on adding one person a month. This takes effort and commitment to the purpose and efficacy of the Wheel of meaning-ful life.)

1. _____
2. _____
3. _____
4. _____
5. _____
6. _____
7. _____
8. _____

B. Call them up TODAY and let them know how important they are to you.
C. Offer yourself to be in their Ring of Intimacy.
D. Schedule a fun activity just for the two of you.

FIGURE 4.2. Ring of intimacy.

Spousal unions are always governed by conditions and usually have real or perceived benefits for the couple involved. But the relationships in the Ring of Intimacy are beyond spousal intimacy. They are pure and beyond any suspicion of personal gain. The mutual sharing is extremely personal, and the commitment is without any conditions.

> The greatest challenge of the day is: how to bring about a revolution of the heart, a revolution which has to start with each one of us.
>
> —*Dorothy Day*

We are able to share with this special ring of intimates our most personal feelings and secret thoughts, and we trust them as completely as we would trust our personal therapist or private lawyer. These special chosen few support, love, and care for us unconditionally. These wonderful intimate friends will not prejudge our feelings nor will they question our actions. They will listen to us and share in our joys and sorrows with deep empathy. These individuals are the people we can turn to in our darkest moments of despair, when we have nowhere else to go. They will rejoice with us, free of envy, and share in our greatest triumphs, achievements, and successes.

People who support you often possess one or more of the following characteristics:

- They are happy to hear from you and chat with you anytime.
- They will travel a great distance to be at your side when you need them.
- They celebrate with you; your achievements are their joys.
- They suffer with you; your pains are also their sorrows.
- You share your most intimate thoughts and feelings with them.
- They do not hesitate to confront you emotionally and intervene when they see you stray.
- They are the people with whom you can stay with when in need.
- They will be happy to accept a collect call from you anytime, anywhere.
- They promote your causes and support your dreams.

Do you have such a circle of support? If so, consider yourself fortunate. If not, then you need start developing one at once. If you have not developed such a ring, maybe it is because you have not shared enough of your intimate self to others. Perhaps you were not open enough to ask others for help and support when you needed them. Ask yourself when and to whom you have offered or lent support in their moments of crisis. How often have others come to you for help and how did you respond to them?

This ring of intimates needs to be nurtured and promoted. Do not wait until a crisis takes place. This nurturing takes time, energy, and even resources. How many individuals can we identify in our ring? Many of us rely on just one person—our spouse. This is a critical shortcoming. In life, we need more than one intimate person. Try to identify at least six to eight persons. They can be members of your family, relatives, colleagues, friends, etc. And remember, this intimate relationship is mutual. There should be a high degree of reciprocity. Otherwise, it will cool off soon. We must be willing to support them, as they are inclined to help us at all costs.

Search deep into your soul and recognize that there is no human intimacy unless we possess esteem for the other person. In life, we all need an intimate ring of support.

☐ Key Concepts in This Chapter

1. Unrealistic expectations of love cause trouble. Love brings both joy and pain to self and others simultaneously.
2. Blindness in love is a chosen cognitive distortion.
3. Human intimacy and relationship is based on other-esteem.
4. Your Ring of Intimacy needs to be nurtured and supported.

5

Developing the Ring of Friendship

"When others are in need, one should extend a helping hand."
—Chinese Roots of Wisdom

General Colin Powell, the Chairman of the Joint Chiefs of Staff during Desert Storm (the Persian Gulf War), once told the story of an 18-year-old private assigned to the war. The private had said during a television interview that he was not afraid and not worried because he was with family. He pointed to his platoon buddies and said, "We are going to take care of each other."

During war, especially in the trenches, there is no individuality. Soldiers are well trained to protect one another, to respect each other, and to count on each other's help and support under any circumstances. This kind of support is critical to survival. It is other-esteem under another guise.

In life, however, too many of us are loners. We have not been taught to rely on and support one another. We do not have friends whom we can count on to lighten the burdens of life. We count on ourselves alone, but when we are in a crisis, the self is insufficient.

We must learn how to take care of each other. We need to discover and build our own support system, our own platoon of buddies who will take care of each other. We need to learn and practice other-esteem.

In life, we all need a ring of support like the soldiers. At times, we find ourselves fighting in a war of human relationships. We do not know where to go or which way to turn, and we wonder about sources, support, and help should we decide to seek assistance. What we need is a Ring of Friendship—a group of supportive friends whom we can count on consistently. This ring of support consists of people with whom we have developed, nurtured, and maintained close friendships of understanding and support over the years (see Figure 5.1).

> Today is meaningful only because there is a tomorrow. Plan for tomorrow's togetherness, today.
> —*Phil Hwang*

This Ring of Friendship usually consists of ten or so close friends, family, relatives, and professional colleagues with whom you have bonded. The relationships are developed over the years and require commitment and mutual sharing in terms of time, resources, and significant life events.

Establishing this ring of support is neither easy nor automatic. If we do not possess such a ring of support, it may be because our focus has been on self and not on others. Several factors have prevented many of us from forming the deep and lasting friendships that sustain us through our lives. We may be convinced that we can do it on our own and that we do not need others. We may have unrealistic expectations of ourselves or others. In today's hectic and stressful environment, some may not feel they have time or need to pursue and maintain friendships. But mutual support is vital to our health and well-being, and without it most of us would have problems surviving periods

---

1. Share common philosophy, goals, or interests in life.
2. Often belong to the same church or service club.
3. Know you and your family well, and are often at social gatherings.
4. Plan events together, such as attend ballgames, theater, etc.
5. Will offer to bring you to the airport.
6. Will help you pack boxes for a move.
7. Send cards or flowers to cheer you up when you are sick.
8. Lend you their car or drive you around when yours is in the shop.
9. Babysit your children or watch your house when you are away.
10. Lend a sympathetic ear during times of personal distress.
11. Share your personal joy and successes in professional life.
12. Offer honest and sincere advice and suggestions when asked.

FIGURE 5.1. Characteristics of friends likely to form a successful ring of friendship.

of pain and suffering. The time, resources, and energy invested in nurturing our rings of support can be life's most rewarding and important investment.

☐ Mutuality in Life Partnerships

A pattern of mutual need permeates through all aspects of our lives. Regardless of where we are—at home, school, or work—we are social creatures. As such, we have a mutual need for each other. It is through mutual sharing and caring that we can achieve happiness and overcome the difficulties we encounter in our daily lives. Our emotional, psychological, and economic well being is largely dependent on our willingness to give and receive, to love and be loved, and to need and be needed.

Social interaction with others is what shapes our lives. Human beings are social creatures, and most of the human life cycle can be defined as a series of relationships. Regardless of the prevailing emphasis on independence, autonomy and individualism in our society, few people will deny the centrality of relationships in our lives.

Life begins with our relating to our mother, then our father, and then the rest of the family. When we were young, a parent-child relationship was naturally developed, along with rivalry and a struggle for adult attention if there were siblings. As we started schooling, a different kind of relationship with another adult took place. At the same time, we started other kinds of interactions with fellow students. Later on, relationships expanded to include more schoolmates, friends, teachers, co-workers, and ultimately an intense close relationship with one's life partner and children. The perception of self develops with interactions and experiences during these early contacts with others. It continues as one grows and matures. It is these series of relationships throughout life that define and add to our self-identity.

It is during these early years that the young mind easily absorbs whatever is presented to it. The promotion of the self is

> With what you get from others, you make a living for yourself. What you give to others, makes a life for yourself.
> —*Hindu saying*

prevalent in society. Child rearing focuses on the development of the individual, but rarely does the meaning or importance of other take a prominent role. The levels of esteem for self and other that the child brings to school come primarily from learning experiences in the home. These experiences and perceptions continue to mold the child during early school days and are reinforced by the added influence of classmates and teachers.

☐ Hi-Tech Living

The material world that we live in has a great impact on us. Every new gadget or invention provides us with an ever greater degree of self-sufficiency and independence. We have gained tremendous benefits from revolutions in high technology. Most of us would agree that our lives have been improved as a result of technology. However, there is a negative side that comes with the advancement of technology. The consequences of this negative side-effect are subtle and not easily identified.

The primary purpose of machines is to help us function better in the workplace and to make our lives more enjoyable. Machines were created to take over the tedious, detailed, and redundant chores of human existence and to release human beings to pursue more creative and enjoyable goals. We built machines to be different from us. They do not need to be motivated and happy to produce results. They do not become bored when repetitious and redundant tasks are given to them. Machines only do what they are told, but they do so, for the most part, efficiently and often perfectly.

Look around you. Identify all parts of your life that have been influenced by the mechanistic metaphor. Think of how much we depend on machines to run our lives. Think of how society is organized. Almost all social institutions are very mechanistic and rationally organized. Organizations and companies are filled with hierarchy and rank. This model was adapted from the military and pervades the educational, public, private, non-profit, and academic sectors of society. Think of how we are increasingly pressured to be more efficient through specialization and mass-production.

> We have become immersed in a world of high-tech perfectionism and efficiency that conflicts with the low-tech nature of meaningful life.
> —*Phil Hwang*

tion. Think of how we are expected to treat employees and subordinates as objects, not as individual human beings. Then you will realize how compartmentalized and mechanistic you have become.

Slowly and insidiously we have incorporated the mechanistic and high-tech character of our material surroundings into our personal relationships. If we are not careful, as we interact and function within an environment filled with rational machines and systems, we subconsciously begin to think of ourselves, our families and our associates as sharing the same attributes of those high-tech machines—slick, slim, efficient, near-perfect, and almost indestructible. And we begin to expect them to function in the same manner—to be rational and mechanical, super-fast, with great accuracy, making few mistakes and possessing the ability to absorb large chunks of information in micro seconds. We have become immersed in a world of high-tech perfectionism that conflicts with the low-tech nature of human beings.

☐ Expectation of Self

Movies, print media, even the toy industry have given us models of physical beauty and perfection that are unrealistic and unhealthy to attempt to achieve. This is not a perfect world. None of us can achieve this level of perfection physically, psychologically, and intellectually. We are blemished human beings living in an imperfect world.

We expect humans to be as infallible as the machines and toys that surround us, and we then develop a higher degree of impatience and intolerance toward ourselves and others. What we forget in today's fast-paced world is that human beings are neither perfect nor perfectly rational beings. In *Thick Face, Black Heart* (1992), Chin-Ning Chu uses the term "imperfect perfection," a phrase that might well apply in this situation. We are not infallible, high-tech inventions. In fact, it has taken millions of years for the human species to evolve to the present point. Thus, we are neither modern nor near-perfect, and we fail miserably in competition with super-efficient machines. But our human limitation in efficiency and perfection is offset by our capability to learn, feel, create, and reason.

Our diminished degree of tolerance for our own imperfections and limitations can torment us. Having unrealistic self-expectations might lead us to irrationally conclude that we are worthless. If, however, each of us believes and accepts the reality that we, as human beings, have inherent limitations, we would then be able to set more realistic goals, with interim steps for success for both our personal and professional achievements. With more realistic and attainable goals, we would then be regularly reinforced with feelings of accomplishment and satisfaction with each goal that we achieve. Our success would motivate and inspire us to vigorously tackle our next objective.

The most humbling attitude we can have in acknowledging our own human limitations is our ability to accept our own mortality. In theory, we know that all living creatures are mortal and will eventually die. Many of us choose to ignore our mortality, however, and careen through life in a spectacularly carefree and careless manner. We ignore our mental health by not learning to handle stress and emotional upheavals. We ignore our physical health by not paying attention to diet, exercise, and physical habits. Some of us choose to abuse our bodies with alcohol and drugs, as if to test their own indestructibility.

Unfortunately, unlike the products we create or produce, there is no warranty of perfection, no guarantee of a specific life span, no refund or exchange. We need to accept ourselves and remind ourselves of the fragile and sensitive casing that houses our mind and soul. We need to take care of our bodies and nourish them so that both mind and body can flourish. A humble acceptance of our mortality will greatly benefit—and probably increase—our time here on earth.

The next important step is to rethink our expectations of other people's opinions. There is no reason to feel paranoid about what other people think of us. We cannot be responsible for anyone else's thoughts, emotions, or actions, and they should not be responsible for ours. We must realize that it is not possible for everyone to love us, nor is it reasonable to expect others to approve of everything we do. We need to give ourselves permission to acknowledge that there are things we do not know or understand. The constant striving for perfection is a fault, not a virtue. This is not an excuse to stop trying to grow or improve ourselves. Everyone should endeavor to learn more and grow as a person; however, it is unhealthy to expect perfection all the time. We need to acknowledge our own imperfections and have the courage to be imperfect. We cannot and should not expect perfection from ourselves, nor can we demand or expect it from others.

☐ Expectations of Others

How many times in work situations have we become frustrated with the shortcomings of our employees, associates, and colleagues, to the point that we convince ourselves the only way to accomplish a job to our satisfaction is to do it ourselves? This is a reflection of our unrealistic expectations, and this kind of thinking and action produces negative results.

This attitude of taking over and doing everything ourselves can breed strong resentment in the workplace and eventually have negative consequences for the company. By not letting workers do the job they were hired to do, we are setting up a troublesome cycle. When we take over someone's task, we take away responsibility and accountability. Without responsibility, the worker will not be committed to the work or to the company. This is no way to motivate and develop workers to their full potential so that the company, in the long run, will benefit. Instead, we are de-motivating our employees and preventing them from developing to their full potential. The same principle applies in our homes. When we try to do everything for everybody, their motivation or desire to try will quickly fade. Why should they attempt anything when we are willing to do everything for them anyway? The main point to remember is that once we are able to accept and believe that we are not perfect, we are more readily able to accept the imperfection of others.

I am not advocating mediocrity or discouraging high standards. But, the often-ignored fact is that this is an imperfect world inhabited by imperfect human beings. Awareness of these limitations should inspire us to set up realistic and attainable goals in life. The constant striving for and attaining of reachable goals are great human motivators and can be a source of great satisfaction and joy throughout life.

The degree of tolerance and acceptance for our own and each other's imperfections, faults, or shortcomings is directly related to our own humility and ability to be a more lovable person. The more understanding and tolerant we are, the more approachable and lovable we are. The daily stress and minor hassles we experience will be reduced considerably. This change in attitude towards realizing and accepting human imperfections will take time and courage. But it will set us free.

☐ "Hello-Goodbye" Friendships

The desire for quick solutions and fast relief from physical discomforts noted in previous chapters is also evident in our human relationships. Just as there are "Hello-Goodbye Marriages," there are also "Hello-Goodbye Friendships." We can quickly and easily become acquainted with each other, and just as easily and quickly forget each other. How many times have we offered broad smiles, firm handshakes, and effusive greetings during an introduction to a stranger, only to walk away five minutes later having already forgotten the person's name? How many times have we said to an acquaintance, "Hey, let's do lunch sometime" or "I will call you next week"? Have we followed up on our words, or are these mere colloquial utterances that should not be taken seriously?

This non-purposeful socialization happens often. Is it any wonder that some people have so many one-night sexual flings or meaningless extramarital affairs? With the philosophy of "here today, gone tomorrow," it is no surprise that people look for situations that offer little complication or involvement. These kinds of FIRES relationships have little foundation or purpose in our personal life. They do not add any value or meaning other than to satisfy our "animal instincts."

> I do not think that the measure of a civilization is how tall its buildings of concrete are, but rather how well its people have learned to relate to their environment and fellow man.
> —*Sun Bear*
> *of the Chippewa Tribe*

The opposite of Hello-Goodbye Friendships is a relationship based on the principles of other-esteem. Other-esteem in the Ring of Friendship demands that we respect the friend and the friendship. Other-esteem is also the fundamental principle on which the qualities of relationships are evaluated.

☐ Pioneering Self-Sufficiency

As discussed in Chapter 1, although we have progressed far beyond the lifestyle of the early rugged pioneers who settled this country, we still place an extraordinary value on self-sufficiency. Some degree of self-sufficiency is good for everyone, but self-sufficiency taken too far means building mental walls, distrusting others, and feeling that we are safe only if we are stronger, wealthier, and more successful than the rest. This distrust of others makes us intolerant of their shortcomings and limitations and insensitive to their needs. An insistence on total self-sufficiency distances us from others and prevents us from building true and intimate friendships. Our eyes and hearts are closed to the discovery of new horizons through the experience of making new friendships. Because each of us is unique, it is through our friendships with other people that we gain new perspectives on life and the world.

☐ Society of Portable Roots

Another factor that prevents us from forming deep friendships is the mobility of the population. Our social structure is based on an extremely mobile population. Demographics show that people living in the west are apt to be more mobile that their counterparts in the east or midwest. One out of every four Californians moves each year. With such constant moving about, how can we possibly establish deep, nourishing roots in our communities? As a result, we are only able to establish "hello friendships." Like migratory birds, we move along with predictable frequency; we do not remain in one neighborhood long enough to nurture personal, long-lasting friendships or build networks of support in our schools, churches, businesses, and other social circles.

Why are Americans so mobile? Why can't we stay in one place long enough to build relationships? The answer is because in this society, an individual's career and professional success have taken precedence over family and community needs. So intent are we upon moving up the ladder of success that we are willing to periodically uproot our families and relocate wherever our company sends us. We delude ourselves that our children will adjust and that friendships and relationships are not important or that they are easy to replace. Our mobile lifestyle only allows us to meet casual acquaintances and establish shallow friendships.

Even within the home, the effects of individualism and self-sufficiency are apparent. In the past, family members used to do things together. Every night, the family ate dinner together, and spent time together after dinner and on the weekends. Now, although we may be sharing the same house, we pursue different activities in different rooms and function quite comfortably as individuals. We all have our own interests and friends and would rather spend time with them than be with our families.

☐ Alone in the Midst of Others

In recent years, "cocooning" has become a popular term with the young adult generation. It refers to a more simple and conservative lifestyle—"cocooning" oneself or staying within the confines of one's home. I first heard of this term from a young friend whose sister and brother-in-law had just purchased their first home. With real estate prices skyrocketing a few years ago, it became increasing difficult for young adults to purchase a home of their own, especially if they lived in California. For those who could scrape together enough money for a down payment, their mortgage payments were so high that they had to cut back drastically on their other expenses, specifically entertainment and vacations. Instead of buying fancy cars, going out to eat all the time, and taking costly vacations each year, new homeowners are now staying at home much more. They spend most of their spare

time doing home improvement projects, working in the yard and garden, relearning the pleasures of cooking, and making use of their
VCRs. The result of cocooning is a further withdrawal of people from
society and their communities. My friend's sister felt proud of her and
her husband's self-sufficiency and was content to devote all of her
spare time to home projects. Needless to say, my friend saw a lot less
of her sister, who had become too busy to socialize with family and
friends on a regular basis.

☐ Interdependence

Because individuality and self-identity are derived from our relationships with others, there is an interconnectedness between ourselves
and society. The actions of other people—whether they are family,
friends, or colleagues—can greatly influence our own thoughts and
actions. The same can be said for our own actions. What we say and
do can have far-reaching effects on those around us. It is this interre-
lationship and interdependency among individuals that holds society
together. We, as a society, need to become more aware of the mutual
influence of individuals on one another. If we are to avoid the pitfalls
of selfishness and egocentricity, we first have to understand that we
do not operate or exist in a vacuum and, second, that our behavior
has negative consequences for many besides ourselves.

Why do we often wait for illness or the death of someone dear to us
before we show affection, concern, or offer assistance to them? When
family and friends are well, we may have the tendency to ignore them
or show only limited contact and connectedness. But when critical
illness strikes, we dash to the scene and offer whatever solace or help
we can. At the time of a death, we gather around with giant doses of
sympathy and attention. But after the ceremonies and a period of
mourning the loss, most of us withdraw into our own lives again,
lapsing back into our shells of self-centeredness until another illness
or death forces us out. We can be of help to each other much more by
avoiding the ups and downs of temporary concern and embracing a
more constant caring attitude in our daily lives. As Robert Frost wrote,
"All those who try to go it solely alone, too proud to be beholden for
relief, are absolutely sure to come to grief."

☐ Sharing Based on Free Choice

The mutual sharing of self and others must be based on personal free
choice and should not have strings attached. This could become a

pitfall that we sometimes fail to see, and at times, we blame others for falling into this guilt trap. Doing things out of obligation instead of personal choice can be called the "what's in it for me" phenomenon (otherwise known as the "you owe me!" debt collection). But, no one should be obligated to do anything unless one freely chooses to—not out of sympathy, not out of loyalty, and definitely not just to get something back.

> Our emotional, psychological and economic well being is largely dependent on our willingness to give and receive, to love and be loved, and to need and be needed.
> —*Phil Hwang*

In our society, we have come to expect something in return for our giving to one another. Even charitable institutions give tax receipts in exchange for our unwanted items. We give something and receive something in return— a quid pro quo arrangement. But does not true goodwill mean giving without the expectation of receiving anything in return? If so, is a quid pro quo arrangement truly an act of goodwill? When are we able to practice other-esteem without expectation of reward or acknowledgment?

As a university professor and counselor, I have heard of numerous incidents of the "what's in it for me" phenomenon. For instance, James asks Cathy out for dinner and a movie. He spends about $50 for the evening . . . no small amount for a full-time college student. When James takes Cathy back to her dorm, he expects or even demands some emotional "goodwill" in return for his evening's "investment." This certainly creates a complicated scenario, and, sadly, Cathy may herself feel that James is entitled to something and that she is "obligated" to comply. How many people like James and Cathy are there in our society?

What is doubly sad about the James-Cathy situation is an erroneous perception by James that he is entitled to certain goodwill, and that an erroneous perception by Cathy that she is somehow obligated to comply against her wishes. In an other esteem-based society, no one demands, feels obligated, or thinks they must give anything. True giving is done from the heart and not out of obligation. If we respond on demand or because of obligation, we may feel we are not responsible for our actions. Then, if something bad happens, we blame the other party for the consequences.

Of course the "benefits" given or demanded vary from person to person and from situation to situation. The important point, however, is that we need to learn how to respond differently from that which is "expected" or "demanded." Actions must be based on what we want to do and not what we feel we have to do. No goodwill should be expected, demanded, or owed by anybody. Our decisions should be based solely on personal choice and not on presumed obligations and unjustified feelings of guilt. When other-esteem exits, we give freely to one another without any expectation or obligation attached.

☐ Steps to Interdependency

John Naisbett, in his best-selling book, *Megatrends* (1982), sends a powerful message: as we progress towards a high-tech society, there will be a corresponding increase in demand for personal "high-touch" relationships. The inference is that our emotional and psychological well-being can be improved by sharing personal burdens.

How do we go about developing our sense of interconnectedness? The solution may be simple in theory, but difficult to implement. We must not let the wishes of the individual take precedence over the needs of the community. There needs to be a delicate balance between the two. First, the family as an institution is in sore need of support and resources. Over the past few decades, the high divorce rate, lack of dependable child care facilities, decreased government funding of social welfare services, and our engrossment with the pursuit of success have wreaked havoc with the American family. One example of the confusing and contradictory messages we receive from our government concerns the federal income tax regulations. On the one hand, government officials in campaign speeches often deplore the high divorce rate in this country, while on the other hand, the government is penalizing people for staying married. Married people have to pay thousands of dollars more each year in taxes—the so-called marriage penalty—than those who are single.

Second, we need to re-establish our sense of community and realize that we are partially accountable and responsible for our social ills. By our inaction and silence, we have permitted our families, communities, and society to fall apart. We need to stay in touch with current events and establish relationships with others in our communities. We need to volunteer and support good causes that benefit us and our communities, and speak out against causes we believe to be negative or harmful to the well-being of our families and communities. Ignorance of a problem is not an acceptable excuse for our lack of involvement.

Finally, we need to learn how to work together. Instead of a nation of individuals focusing on vast and varied differences, we need to acknowledge and learn from our differences, and concentrate on discovering similarities and working toward common goals. Cognitive distortions cause us to view the world in a win-lose perspective. With cooperation and interdependence, we can achieve outcomes where nobody loses and everyone benefits.

> It is through our friendships with other people that we gain new perspectives on life and the world.
> —*Phil Hwang*

☐ Developing Our Rings of Support

Our Ring of Intimacy, Ring of Friendship (see Figure 5.2), and the third Ring of Support are vital to our social adjustment and our physical and mental well-being. All are critically important as we progress down the

A. Identify your personal support system by listing as many people as possible in your Ring of Friendship.

1. _____
2. _____
3. _____
4. _____
5. _____
6. _____
7. _____
8. _____
9. _____
10. _____

B. Call them up TODAY and let them know how important they are to you.
C. Offer yourself to be in their Ring of Friendship.
D. Schedule a fun activity just for the two of you.
E. If you are unable to fill the above Ring of Friendship, work on adding one person a month. This takes effort and commitment to the purpose and efficacy of the Wheel of Meaningful Life.

FIGURE 5.2. Ring of friendship.

path of life. Without them, happiness and meaningful life would be elusive.

Once we have changed our attitude and accepted the importance of other-esteem and mutual dependency in our lives, how do we go about building our rings of support?

First, identify and categorize your support network. On a piece of paper write down a tentative list of names underneath each of the two rings of support. One way to begin adding names to your list and to support your community at the same time is to become involved in a support or service group, such as Kiwanis, Rotary, etc. Members of these clubs are people who like to have fun together, enjoy traveling to foreign countries, perform meaningful tasks as a group, and share a little bit of the self to one another in a warm and supportive environment.

Think about the people on your lists; spend time and thought on creating the lists. Next, spend the next six to eight months cultivating and nurturing these people to determine if they regard you in the same light that you regard them. Some names may shift from one group to another, and some may end up off your lists altogether. But after eight months of thinking and observing, you will be able to arrive at a final selection.

Once you feel your two primary lists are complete, it is essential that you constantly make an effort to enrich the respective relationships. A college friend or an ex-next-door neighbor whom you have not seen in over six months does not belong on either the first or second ring lists. These two rings of people will be fluid, not static. Some names will be dropped and other will be added due to environmental and life event changes. Developing these rings of support does not entail the waving of a magic wand, but involves a well-thought-out, methodical approach to life. Your happiness—even your survival—rests on the choice you make to switch from the "I" mentality to the "We" way of thinking. You are who you are because of other people.

The Ring of Friendship, the Ring of Intimacy, and the third Ring of Support are not just for emergencies or crises in our lives. Although it is comforting to know that they are there when we may need them, they are not just the emergency crews of our lives, like our neighborhood firefighter units, waiting for the 9_1_1 call.

These two groups of phenomenal people play an even greater role as our mentors, guides, and colleagues in our daily living, experiencing, and learning. With them and through them, we learn to appreciate the daily routines of living and the ecstasies of success and achievement. These two groups will also convey to us at different times the significance and requirements of devotion and esteem (see Figure 5.3).

Evaluate yourself on the following characteristics of relationship with others. Circle the number on right which most closely describe your present attitude, feelings or behavior.

1 = Never   2 = Sometimes   3 = Usually   4 = Always

	Never	Sometimes	Usually	Always
1. Do you celebrate others' successes and promotions?	1	2	3	4
2. Do you demonstrate concern and care for others' welfare?	1	2	3	4
3. Do you believe and practice that others have the same rights?	1	2	3	4
4. Do you acknowledge others' individuality and accept shortcomings?	1	2	3	4
5. Do you promote others' dreams and causes?	1	2	3	4
6. Do you understand individual differences in perception?	1	2	3	4
7. Do you develop an extensive Ring of Friendship?	1	2	3	4
8. Do you become a member of someone else's Ring of Friendship?	1	2	3	4
9. Are you conscious of the consequences of one's behavior on others?	1	2	3	4
10. Are you able to forgive others and move on with your own life?	1	2	3	4
11. Do you accept personal responsibility for one's own behavior?	1	2	3	4
12. Do you avoid blaming others for "accidents" in life?	1	2	3	4

FIGURE 5.3. Other-esteem in relationships.

All of these members of our rings become very much a part of our "extended" family.

   This is what other-esteem is all about. Two rings to make up a wheel of meaningful life. The Ring of Intimacy and the Ring of Friendship. We need them just as they need us. These are rings of social support. Select them carefully and deliberately. Now is the time for you to make your choice. Alter your point of view and act purposely. Which is it to be? Individualism or interdependence?

☐ Key Concepts in This Chapter

1. Others are lovable, imperfect beings too.
2. Increase your level of tolerance and acceptance of others.
3. Learn to think differently and act purposely.
4. Practice human interdependency and esteem of others.
5. Develop your ring of friendship support system.

Other-Esteem and Leadership

"I am a self-made millionaire."

—Anonymous company president

Not long ago, I interviewed the president of a small manufacturing company, which he had started from scratch over 10 years earlier. He proudly informed me that he was a self-made millionaire. I looked straight into his eyes and in a solemn voice asked, "Are you telling me that during all these 10 years you worked in the company by yourself?" He was silent for a long while. I made my point. This man's realization of the importance of employer and employee interdependence will make him a better leader and manager. If he truly believed in the concept of self-made success, he would understand his dependency on his employees' contribution to his success. Without this realization, he does not possess any degree of other-esteem.

The concepts and practice of other-esteem are nowhere more wanting and vitally needed than in the world of work. Respect, acceptance, and the appreciation of others within the work environment are extensions of who we are. Many are caught up in competition, jealousy, and the pursuit of individual goals and achievements. Some look at their present occupation as a temporary step to another personal advancement. Other-esteem in the workplace demands the understanding and belief in inter-dependency—how to share credits, successes, and achievements of work-related projects. There is no room for self-aggrandizing.

Our impatient nature—Fast Instant Relief Syndrome (FIRES), as defined in Chapter 1—is also evident in our attitude towards money and finances. We often carry this short-sighted attitude into the businesses we run and work in. We are very present-oriented, emphasizing the "here and now" approach to running and selling company products and services. While American companies have tended to focus on the short term, other business cultures appear to be more patient and future-oriented.

> We must learn that we need each other to succeed. There are no self-made leaders. There are no self-made millionaires.
>
> —*Phil Hwang*

This short-term meaningful vision has cost American businesses billions of dollars in lost business and failed opportunities. By not planning for the medium and long term, we have allowed the Japanese and other Asian economies to overtake us in many key industries. How has this come about? It is often because American companies' number one priority is to its stockholders: a company's financial status is determined by its quarterly return on investment. Therefore, due to the way our economy is structured, companies have focused most of their resources and energies towards short-term profits and gains. But in many instances, short-term profits and long-term planning are conflicting priorities. Executives who concern themselves with fast, immediate profit for the stockholders will not set aside huge budgets for the research and development that will be necessary for future growth.

On an individual level, our attitudes towards money are not much better than those in the workplace. The U.S. national savings rate is much lower than most other industrialized countries, and our national consumer debt is now beyond the hundred billion dollar mark. Why is this debt so high? Not surprisingly, it is because of our society's instant gratification lifestyle. Most people are impatient and not willing to wait. They want something and they want it NOW, regardless of whether or not they have the money.

We have become a credit card society, with everything bought on credit—from houses, cars, and furniture, to clothes, medical services, food, and travels. We are seduced by clever advertisers who tell us, "Buy now and pay later," but who do not remind us that the catch is the huge interest charged for the privilege of paying later.

Unscrupulous individuals, cognizant of our impatient nature, have made untold millions off our weakness. Always on the lookout for a shortcut to wealth and riches, a large number of Americans are taken advantage of each year by phony, get-rich-quick schemes. These scams have occurred with increasing frequency over the past decade. Why are they working? And why do people fall for them time and time again? This vulnerability is caused by the FIRES syndrome at work again—delusions that one can succeed without hard work, time, and energy. Just as in the business world, planning for the long term and patiently working toward goals and financial security would not leave one vulnerable to seduction by short-term scams.

☐ "Hello-Goodbye" Business

The "hello-goodbye" attitude discussed in the previous chapters is also reflected in the way many workers approach their relationship with their places of employment. Many business people are interested only in making the fast buck and achieving the quick promotion. They are not concerned with either a long-term company relationship or establishing a reputation of loyalty. They change companies whenever they can find someone to pay a higher salary and provide a better position. Their minds are set on a short-term plan. They do not make any attempt to cultivate lasting relationships with their companies.

This "hello-goodbye" behavior is based purely on self-interest and the attainment of individual objectives. Organizations also suffer from this high mobility. Colleagues suffer too as projects are left on hold until a replacement is hired. At times, unethical staff members even take sensitive data, files, etc., for personal profit or to impress a new employer. These "me first" decisions ignore the effect on others.

There is a need to see the business world anew and to attain a different perspective of employer-employee relationships. Due to economic downturns and the down-sizing of many corporations, business executives are looking for advice. Companies are looking at new theories of leadership development simply because there is a different configuration of the labor force. Organizations are taking new looks at the process of "re-engineering." Consultants and experts in management and leadership are coming out with new theories and blueprints for improvements of the old system and way of doing things. But perhaps there is a better way to look at organizations. It may be that, rather than re-inventing the wheel, a wheel is not what is needed at all. A fresh look at re-organization, the basic principles of leadership, relationship, work ethics, and personal and organizational development may result in a completely new way of doing business, of running a company, and of producing goods and providing services.

Over the past two decades, American society has bluntly roared way beyond the Industrial or Post-Industrial Age and into a new era: the

Information Age. No longer is one person capable of creative, long-lasting changes within an organization. U.S. products and services are no longer accepted blindly without question or challenge. There are radical changes in our diversified and expanded client base. With new countries opening their doors to American products and services, there are profound effects of global economy on our business organizations. Colleagues and subordinates join companies with a huge variety of education levels, attitudes, skills, and life experiences. These are all critical factors of the Information Age that demand a vital and comprehensive model of organizational relationship.

A new model for organizational transformation and leadership evolution, the "Loop Paradigm," takes all these elements into consideration. The Loop Paradigm is a moving away from the self-focused to a balanced relationship of self and other in the world of work. It is a dynamic model of organizational effectiveness in leadership based on the theory of other-esteem, of Yin and Yang balance and harmony, of interdependence, and of togetherness in an organization for mutual benefit and shared purposefulness.

The Loop Paradigm for the 21st Century consists of:

- Shared meaningful vision
- Commitment to mutual benefits
- Synergy in teamwork
- Acknowledged interdependency
- Communication and feedback
- Networking externally and internally

A Shared Meaningful Vision

Adlerian psychotherapists believe that all human behavior is purposive. An organization, a collective series of successive and concurrent human behavior, must have a clear and precise purpose for existence. The declaration of the organization's distinct purpose is its meaningful vision statement, which should be both simple in its meaningful elegance and the result of involved group consensus. It must also be other-directed. It cannot be self-serving, vicious, and destructive. Meaningful vision statements must have the following qualitative assertions:

- acknowledgment of interdependency
- determination to provide a harmonious working environment
- noble, altruistic, and benevolent goals
- cooperative and supportive management and colleagues

- focus in goal attainment
- total commitment to multiculturalism
- commitment to a specific client base
- unique and rational purpose for existence

Frequently, the president or person who started the organization is the visionary—the only person who knows or remembers the rationale for its being. However, it is not enough that the CEOs and the top management alone understand the direction or goal of the company. The visionary must convey this excitement of purpose and focus to all who are part of the organization. Everyone in each division and unit of the company must be part of this decision-making process and must understand and totally embrace it. Otherwise, each individual worker will be pursuing his own agenda rather than the organizational objectives.

By its very essence, meaningful vision is future-oriented. Therefore, those who work to create the meaningful vision of the organization must be visionaries or futurists who understand both social and cultural changes, have the ability to think impassionately, re-evaluate present meaningful visions, and effect changes when environments and circumstances demand.

A meaningful vision statement must be dynamic and periodically

There are many fine examples of meaningful vision statements throughout the business and professional world. One such statement can be found in the Ben and Jerry's Company, which they say is "dedicated to the creation and demonstration of a new concept of linked prosperity." Their statement consists of three parts—product, economic, and social—but as they state: "Underlying the mission is the determination to seek new and creative ways of addressing all three parts, while holding a deep respect for individuals inside and outside the company and for all the communities of which they are a part."

re-evaluated, questioned, and perhaps even modified. Thus, as the world changes, so must the meaningful vision of any organization. Even clients and suppliers fluctuate. It is vital for any organization that wants to survive and prosper to continually examine its rationale for being. Then the meaningful vision must be reality-tested, redirected, and revised to reflect the current role and function of the organization, the workers involved, and the clientele it serves.

To arrive at this meaningful vision, an organization can ask the following questions:

> Why are we doing what we are doing?
> Is there another venue or a better way for our existence?
> Is the world a better place because of who we are and what we are doing?
> Are our workers happy and satisfied because they believe in what they are doing?"

An organization's meaningful vision must be clearly articulated to and understood by other constituents involved with the organization, such as suppliers or clients. Because these groups are external and tangential to the organization, they need not subscribe to the same set of values and goals, but they must understand them so as not do anything to sabotage or compromise the integrity of the employees.

A truly shared meaningful vision is the fundamental first step towards attaining a better other esteem culture within the work environment. Both survival and progress are the products of a collective purposeful action. Colleagues who are infused with this collective enthusiasm and purposeful attitude will come out with a greater feeling of achievement for self, others, and the organization. If all of this takes place in a friendly and positive setting, with employees at all levels willing to work together to solve problems and fix troubled areas, the organization will not only survive, it will grow and prosper.

A Commitment to Mutual Benefits

Besides a commitment to the meaningful visions of the organization by everyone involved, another important aspect of other-esteem in the world of work is mutual commitment between workers to promote the welfare and benefits of *all* within the organization.

Those who are balanced in self- and other-esteem often see their jobs as a career. They are motivated, loyal, and care about the company. They consistently go above and beyond the call of duty and excel in their jobs. Their goals coincide with the company's objectives, and they share with the organization a commitment to those objectives.

If workers are only self-focused, they will be plotting their own path of glory in any organization they join. They see their jobs as merely a paycheck. They do the minimum required and do not really care about the company. Too much individual thinking, non-conformity, and self-centeredness causes friction among colleagues; their association is short and superficial. They may be quick to complain about personal inconveniences and the routine hassles of work, finding fault with every company policy. While there may be many valid complaints, fault-finders rarely come up with solutions to the problems. Their contributions to their colleagues and employer will be minimal, and they may quickly move on to bigger and better things, often leaving their former colleagues to clean up the mess left behind.

Today, many people change companies as easily as they discard an old pair of shoes. In some industries, this practice is not only accepted but expected as a necessity to advancement. Such employees have little or no loyalty to their companies. Many of them perceive their work as a temporary source of income rather than as a place to build a career and plan for the long term. It becomes a place for personal achievements, a temporary stepping stone to something more personally rewarding.

On the other hand, many organizations downsize or "right size" at the expense of loyal and senior employees. These organizations' only concern is about their bottom line. They do not realize or cannot understand that loyalty is a two-way street. Unless the organization, represented by the people in leadership positions, demonstrate caring for their staff, workers in return will not be loyal to the organization.

Team players balance personal achievements and positive contributions to their organizations. Executives take notice of such loyal employees, recognizing and rewarding them accordingly. This is a manifestation of the mutual commitment by all involved.

Managers, presidents, CEOs, and employers should learn and understand their moral, ethical and legal commitment to those who work for them. In many ways, they can affect and influence their employees' financial and emotional stability. By putting their employees needs at the forefront, they can not only increase employee loyalty and enthusiasm, but derive benefit from this in terms of benefits to customers (Rosenbluth, 1994).

Company decisions and policies should not be based on expediency or solely on money concerns without careful regard for the consequences of these actions on employees and their families. By their very leadership, they have also committed themselves to the ethical management of the company resources.

It is interesting to note that many American executives receive a salary and benefits two to three times higher than their Japanese counterparts. Some also receive millions of dollars in bonuses through questionable manipulation of company policies, selling of units or divisions, and massive employee layoffs in order to influence stock prices.

> Leaders who practice the principle of other-esteem will invariably bring success to the organization.
> —*Phil Hwang*

But leaders who practice the basic principle of other-esteem will invariably increase their staff's loyalty and commitment, which in turn results in a stronger company. These officers make themselves available to their colleagues, both personally and professionally, and are sensitive to their staff's attitudes and feelings both in their daily routines and in the roller coaster ride of corporate life.

Unfortunately this attitude is far too infrequent. Not long ago, an employee was laid off by a large defense company only a week after his son was killed in an accident. The company officials explained that this had been planned long before as part of a downsizing program. A policewoman who was wounded during an arrest that turned violent was later fired from the force because she could no longer perform her job. Organizations thoughtlessly implementing policies that harm employee morale and engender distrust of upper level management must share in the blame. Those that observe only the bottom line with no regard to employee welfare and well-being are not giving their employees any incentive to be loyal, motivated, and productive. For instance, companies that purposely fire people just months before they are to receive their retirement benefits (considered a "cost saving measure") are instigating deep distrust, antipathy, and revolt from the lowest level on up.

It is true that sometimes organizations must let go of workers for a variety of valid reasons. In these cases, they should offer counseling, employment opportunities, and re-training programs to employees who must be let go. Such a show of support will go a long way towards building an atmosphere of mutual trust and respect.

If executives function with a "throw away" attitude, the entire company will sink into oblivion. Any company with employees who are predominately in the "throw away" mode will experience dwindling sales, dissatisfied customers, and loss of quality control. Those who run such organizations will find themselves mired in low employee morale, high employee turnover, and low productivity. With such a negative attitude, no company or organization can remain competitive, regardless of how talented the CEO or well-financed the corporation. If, however, everyone in a corporation, from top executives down to the lowest level of employees, is in the "fixing" mode, more problems can be solved and new solutions found. The net effect will be a collegial bonding, a togetherness necessary for attaining the shared meaningful vision of the organization.

Mutual commitment also means that everyone in the organization is willing to take on personal responsibility for the successes and failures of the company, unlike what is demonstrated in the following story:

Who's To Blame?
"This is a story about people named Everybody,
Somebody, Anybody, and Nobody.
There was an important job to be done and
Everybody was sure that Somebody would do it.
Anybody could have done it but Nobody did it.
Somebody got angry about that because it was Everybody's job.
Everybody thought Anybody could do it
but Nobody realized that Everybody would not do it.
It ended up that Everybody blamed Somebody
when Nobody did what Anybody could have done."
—Author Unknown

Another example of mutual commitment is the realization of mutual dependency between the organization and its clients. Each group seemingly makes decisions and choices independently of the other. But organizations depend on their loyal clientele for prosperity, survival, and fulfillment of their meaningful visions, and clients rely on the quality products and dedicated services offered by their providers to satisfy their needs and wants of life.

Synergy in Teamwork

Synergy refers to the effort of a group accomplishing objectives that no individual could attain alone. It is a demonstration of the magic of teamwork and the effective power of togetherness, where the whole is greater than the sum of its parts. It is the height of cooperation no individual effort could ever accomplish, so that $1 + 1 + 1 + 1 = 5$ or 7 or possibly 10. It is action, togetherness, and group goal-directed.

Synergy in action is exemplified in sports teams, such as a professional football organization. It recruits different kinds of athletes to play various positions. Some are very big, others are extremely fast; some can throw, others can kick; some are offensive players, and others are defensive players. They all complement each other, and together *as a team* they perform and achieve goals beyond what could be accomplished by an individual.

Since synergy is not based on individual accomplishments or performances, synergy in action is possible only when other-esteem is the prevailing attitude among the participants involved. It means foregoing self-interest and personal goals in favor of the organization's meaningful vision. Everyone who actively participates and contributes to this synergistic activity can derive a sense of personal pride and satisfaction from the effort of the group as a whole.

A company, like a symphony orchestra, is made up of the performances of each individual artist. Each one plays a different instrument, at various times harmonized in tempo and volume. Only the combined efforts of all individuals can yield the beautiful music no single individual can ever hope to produce on his own. At times, the orchestra may feature an individual artist. However, she always acknowledges the other musicians' accompaniments. The featured artist knows full well that the beautiful music everyone is enjoying is effect of synergy.

Look at how many companies and workers are involved in building the Atlas rocket that boosts the space shuttle into space. Thousands of workers in different companies at many locations all produce different parts for the Atlas rocket and its ultimate successful launch. Yet every part must function perfectly for this rocket to achieve its mission. No one could have done it individually. As the rocket roars through the blue sky and into deep space, there is a collective pride and sense of achievement realized by all involved with building the rocket.

Synergy of action applies to every level or structure of the organization. It starts with a committee assigned to a specific task, a team working on a similar project, or a unit or a division with international consequences. Each must be conscious of the synergistic effect of their individual efforts and understand each other's strength and weaknesses so that they can balance and help each other.

Acknowledged Interdependency

In American culture, we learn to be independent and self-sufficient very early in life. Entering the workplace, we experience a different environment with a different set of expectations. We must learn that we need each other to succeed within the organization as well as in our personal lives.

The example of the so-called "self-made millionaire" illustrates the importance of leaders who practice other-esteem and understand interdependency. Interdependency within an organization is the acknowledgment and practice of believing in the vital contribution of each employee within the organization. It is the mutual respect for one another and the support of everyone's role and function from the top CEO down to the lowest salaried personnel in the entire organization. In our society, there is a tendency for some people to discriminate against others who are "lower" than us in the hierarchy. Yet how many executives are lost without their secretaries, assistants, or support personnel who take care of the logistics and keep the organization functioning smoothly. The climate of any organization should be such that it is conducive to both the attainment of the mission of the organization and to individual growth and development at all levels of the organization.

The gurus of leadership speak frequently of "empowerment" as the solution to the problem of top-down management. The irony of empowerment is that the power is bestowed to one person by another. Any power that is given can also be taken away. The only true empowerment is self-empowerment.

Those who do not acknowledge the significance of others' roles are not acting interdependently. It is the workers who produce the excellent products and provide quality services for the entire organization. The leader can only be as good as the followers.

Interdependency affords opportunities for new and divergent learning for those who choose to take advantage of it. In too many organizations, people who have attained positions of power have stopped learning. They want to maintain the status quo and are no longer open to suggestions, innovation, and creativity. They say that they "have arrived" and have paid their dues, and now it's time to relax and enjoy life. Or they are so overwhelmed by their need to micro-manage their operations that they have no time to share and learn. Neither the company nor these executives will prosper or last very long.

> Independent people who do not have the maturity to think and act interdependently may be good individual players, but they won't be good leaders or team players.
> —*Stephen Covey (1989)*

Interdependency is also an exercise in humility. It is humbling sometimes to seek help from colleagues. But if we truly respect each other's role and function within the organization, it will become natural for each one of us to acknowledge and practice interdependency.

Communication and Feedback

Communication is information sharing. When we share information, we also communicate esteem and respect to other people. The second part of the communication loop, however, is feedback. While it is important to share, it is just as vital to seek and receive feedback. Communication without input or feedback is dictatorial and shows a lack of respect for the intelligence of others. The completion of the communication loop in an open dialogue is a great demonstration of other-esteem.

In this age of high technology, no weakness can cause greater harm than a failure to inform. American society is entering the era of mental power rather than physical ability. More jobs are created that require the use of mental ability than those of brawn and sweat. As workers achieve higher mental functioning and better intellectual reasoning, they demand access to data in order to make better and more rational decisions. This change in the characteristics of the workers requires an equal response in the leadership.

Some leaders think feedback means telling others when they are doing something wrong. However, good leadership understands that communication and feedback are also (and more importantly), about communicating, reinforcing, and focusing on the positive. An individual's behavior can vary greatly depending on the system of rewards and incentives in place. Rewarding positive behavior will reinforce and motivate human beings to achieve greater goals. However, if attention is always focused on an individual's mistakes, errors, and weaknesses, with no rewards for achievements because they are taken for granted, motivation to accomplish goals is lost.

Those who practice other-esteem wait to pounce on others for the slightest mistakes. Instead of trying to catch someone doing a bad job, Ken Blanchard (1982), in his best seller book, *One Minute Manager*, suggests trying to catch others doing a good job. Rewarding positive behavior motivates people and gives them an incentive to accomplish more. In other words, positive reinforcement encourages further success.

Positive feedback is easier to receive for most people, although some have a tendency to discount positive feedback aimed at themselves, particularly those from Asian cultures. When someone is commended for a job well done, the discounted comment might be: "I was just lucky!" A friend compliments someone on a lovely dress. "Oh, I bought this dress on sale at a discount store!" Learn to accept compliments and positive feedback graciously and without any disclaimers. Most positive comments are sincere and genuine, and a cause to feel good. We do not share enough positive feedback with each other. Positive feedback is a natural outgrowth of other-esteem. Share it!

Negative feedback is harder to give and harder to receive. In life, we receive negative feedback both from justifiable and unjustifiable sources. Learn to see the world anew from this feedback. We probably hate to admit it, but much negative feedback may be deserved and valid. Other people have a unique perspective of us and our behaviors that we do not have. They can know about our blind spots, the things about us that we do not realize about ourselves. It shows grace and strength to accept valid negative feedback, thank the person who gives it, and change our lives accordingly.

This loop of communication-feedback covers many different aspects within the work environment. Many companies manipulate and control the expected outcomes of certain decisions, such as staff additions and policy changes, based on the judgments of the selected few. Only after the decisions are made are they communicated to everyone in the organization. In appearance, management may be following the democratic principle of decisions by the committee. However, staff may not be happy because they did not participate in the decision-making process. Were they allowed to give feedback in the communication loop, they might feel and act differently. Communication without feedback is meaningless.

Communication can be enriched when feedback is solicited. Executives, management, colleagues and workers all need to learn how to listen and obtain feedback from each other. Both managerial and collegial attainment and practice of other-esteem demand the delivery and solicitation of both positive and negative feedback. Without honest and sincere feedback, one can become a "bull in a china shop" moving from one disaster to another.

In practice, many programs for training leadership, even among some of the prestigious institutions, still concentrate only on the development of the individual executive, lectures on theories, a variety of exercises and simulations to enhance learning, and acquisition of leadership

> Leaders should facilitate and not mitigate.
> —Phil Hwang

skills (see Figures 6.1 and 6.2). Yet many books, articles, and research publications stress the inadequacy such a one-sided approach. The ever-popular benchmark, "360 Degree Feedback" is a good example:

Evaluate your *workplace* based on the following characteristics related to other-esteem. Circle the number on right which most closely your *organization's* present attitude or behavior.

	1 = Never	2 = Sometimes	3 = Usually	4 = Always
1. Actively demonstrates positive commitment to multiculturalism.	1	2	3	4
2. Endorses and promotes both horizontal and vertical interdependency.	1	2	3	4
3. Creates a harmonious, non-competitive working environment.	1	2	3	4
4. Sets and strives for noble, altruistic, and benevolent goals.	1	2	3	4
5. Employs cooperative and supportive management and colleagues.	1	2	3	4
6. Consistent focus on goal attainment through synergistic actions.	1	2	3	4
7. Commits and supports to a specific client base.	1	2	3	4
8. Clearly defines unique and rational purpose for existence.	1	2	3	4
9. Specific and clear vision shared by all.	1	2	3	4
10. Enthusiastically supports community projects and activities	1	2	3	4
11. Communicates and solicits feedback at all levels.	1	2	3	4
12. Promotes participatory management and shared ownership.	1	2	3	4
13. Leaders are primarily people-oriented.	1	2	3	4

FIGURE 6.1. Other-esteem and leadership, part I.

Evaluate *yourself* on the following characteristics relating to your workplace. Circle the number on right which most closely *your* resent attitude or behavior.

1 = Never   2 = Sometimes   3 = Usually   4 = Always

	1 = Never	2 = Sometimes	3 = Usually	4 = Always
1. I am actively promoting multiculturalism at my place of work.	1	2	3	4
2. I am proud to be identified with or represent my organization.	1	2	3	4
3. I contribute to a harmonious, non-competitive working environment.	1	2	3	4
4. I can identify with the noble, altruistic, and benevolent goals of my firm.	1	2	3	4
5. I actively recruit, support, or promote dedicated colleagues.	1	2	3	4
6. I am committed to goal attainment through synergistic actions.	1	2	3	4
7. I understand that my job is related to the quality of my goods/service.	1	2	3	4
8. I support my organization's unique and rational purpose for existence.	1	2	3	4
9. I understand, share, and support my company's vision.	1	2	3	4
10. I volunteer and support community projects and activities.	1	2	3	4
11. I am open to and provide feedback.	1	2	3	4
12. I take ownership and responsibility in the daily events of my firm.	1	2	3	4
13. I promote my company's products or services to people I meet.	1	2	3	4
14. I take personal responsibility in improving our firm's goods/services.	1	2	3	4
15. I willingly purchase/utilize my organization's goods/services.	1	2	3	4

FIGURE 6.2. Other-esteem and leadership, part II.

the questions are almost all focused on others' perception of the leader. While this is necessary, they do not help the leaders understand anyone else in the organization. Does the leader know their meaningful

> With the best of all leaders,
> When the work is done,
> The project completed,
> The people all say,
> We did it ourselves.
> —*the Tao*

visions, what they value, their fears and frustrations? Leadership is caring for others. Leadership is developing those who are entrusted to us. Leaders need to "have a heart." They must be concerned about service to the community, pro-

moting diversity, and the welfare of their staff. It is giving back what has been received.

Networking Internally and Externally

Other-esteem in the workplace is also manifested by both personal and professional networking, and in a high level of community involvement. Networking is the sharing of oneself and the building of bridges to others, both at personal and professional levels. It is related very closely to effective interpersonal relationships, and can take place in all groups *within* an organization and with professional colleagues *outside* the work place. The sharing of self is giving back to others what we know about ourselves but what others do not know about us.

There are several levels of networking, beginning with *work colleagues*. Within the organization, networking is your safety net. It diminishes the chances of derailment and fosters cooperation, team building, and a high degree of mutual interdependency. Do not limit this networking to your immediate boss and colleagues. Learn how to expand your horizon to as many people as possible, even to someone totally unrelated to the present job and sphere of work environment. You can start with simple coffee talk, without any hidden agenda as a first step in planting a seed for eventual bonding.

The second level of networking is with colleagues *outside the company* who possess similar professional and personal interests. This networking stimulates the mind and continues to sharpen one's knowledge and skills-acquisition. Because this kind of networking is non-competitive, it fosters passion and excitement for work and lowers the possibility of stress and job burnout.

Community is the third level of *networking*. There is no better way to demonstrate other-esteem than community involvement and service. Community involvement demands time, commitment, and should become very much a part of every organization's operation. Sharing one's talent and resources helps to complete the self.

The next level of networking involves the *cooperation* of one company with another. Doing it alone is no longer a viable option for the 21st century. The practice of manufacturing products with parts provided by other companies is not new—the garment and auto industries have been doing this for decades. Today, more companies believe that work and services will be more beneficial if parceled out. These so called "virtual factories" can be very efficient and cost effective. Each company can concentrate on what it does best. This kind of cooperation is based on mutual interdependency and on helping everyone succeed.

This is the opposite of what we are seeing in some large corporate takeovers where companies increase business by buying other companies. They do not provide better services or invent better products. This is simply large business manifestation of power hungry mentality. Cornering the entire market in order to be the largest buying block is a sign of corporate superiority designed to dominate and suppress others.

The final level of networking is *global networking*. As the distance between countries diminishes and the differences between cultures decreases, we need to expand our meaningful vision beyond the boundaries of the oceans. Recent technological advancements in other countries have been extremely impressive. Americans can no longer take a superior attitude or belittle other cultures' achievements and advances in either product and services. Any attitude of supremacy blinds us to opportunities. International networking will expand our awareness and facilitate new learning experiences. We must continue to learn from others. Only "self-sufficient" and "self-made" individuals ever stop learning. Network, keep an open mind, and learn from others.

> We are working another basic outlook: the world as organization. This would profoundly change the categories of our thinking and influence our practical attitudes. We must envision the biosphere as a whole with mutually reinforcing or mutually destructive interdependencies.
> —*Ludwig von Bertalanffy*

Networking does not happen accidentally. First, one must possess a positive attitude and a conviction of its worth. Next comes planning and continuous efforts at implementation. There will be both successes and failures because you can only direct your own attitude, feeling, and behavior, and you cannot dictate the outcome. Networking of all kinds at all levels brings about bonding and fosters both self-esteem and other-esteem.

☐ Key Concepts in This Chapter

1. Focus on self disparages the contributions of others.
2. "Hello-Goodbye" attitude is a self-centered behavior.
3. The Loop Paradigm is a new paradigm for organizations based on other-esteem. It consists of:

   - A dynamic and future-oriented shared meaningful vision
   - Mutual commitment
   - Synergy in action
   - Interdependency
   - Communication involving the sharing of information and receiving feedback
   - Personal and professional.

4. Quality and service first.

Other-Esteem in a Multicultural Society

"The voice of the majority is no proof of justice."
—Johann Von Schiller

"When will you go back home to where you came from?" This is a question posed to me over the years, the implication being that since I do not look like a white Caucasian or was not born in this country, this must not be my home. Annoyed, I usually respond by saying that I have lived longer in this country than any other place. This is my home now!

☐ Accidents of Life

Gender, race, physical appearance, wealth, and social class are all accidents of birth. Since none of us makes these choices, none of us should blame them or take credit for them. It is not our fault or to our credit to be born a white male, of a wealthy and prominent family, or in the U.S. Some are jealous of those who fit these categories. Do you think they do not have problems of their own? Ask them! These factors are no guarantee to happiness in life. It is not our privilege to despise others who arrive in this world different than we are.

Many people evaluate themselves and others' based purely on these accidents of life. Other-esteem looks beyond these accidents and values the essence of the characteristics. One could just as easily have been born in starving Somalia, or a different gender or race, or to a more dysfunctional family. These are not "options" that we can choose or deny. When we realize how randomly one comes to inherit superior or more enviable traits of life, the more humble we become and more hesitant to look down on others who are not as fortunate to have the more desirable accidents of birth.

> Physical appearances, relations, family wealth, gender, etc., are all accidents of life.
>
> —*Phil Hwang*

A colleague of mine at the University of San Diego used to say that we are all one accident or one split second away from being a special, a physically challenged, or disabled person. This realization and attitude towards certain realities of life make us much more sensitive to others who are culturally, physically, economically and ethnically different or more or less fortunate than others. Accept life the way we are live!

☐ Self Is the Basis of Discrimination

An exaggerated sense of self-esteem on the one hand or lack of other-esteem on the other is frequently the basis of racial prejudice and discrimination. An exaggerated sense of self-esteem, the fad of this past decade, is often misused and rationalized—contrary to the spirit and practice of multiculturalism. The lack of other-esteem towards those who are different from us, the promotion of self at the expense of others, the attainment of personal goals, and the disregard of others' achievements underlie much of our discrimination, including racial, gender, and socioeconomic.

As we learned in earlier chapters, Americans often strive to reach their full potential by depending on their uniqueness and individuality. This emphasis on self-identity and self-achievement has gone overboard. A sense of independence and an awareness of one's own heritage and background are important components of establishing one's identity and esteem. However, taken too far, the desire for self-gratification and greed will overshadow the concepts of other-esteem. This includes social responsibility and concern, mutual dependency and cooperation, and a sense of community.

Today, many elements or aspects of American culture, customs, and traditions are falling apart. We have lost a sense of social concern for one another. We no longer stay long enough in a single place to establish roots and build up a feeling of community. Crimes of passion and street violence are daily occurrences in almost every city. There is often an imposed sense of competition, in arenas where there are only win-lose outcomes, for what some feel are scarce resources available for a cleaner environment, more humane political structure, the availability of human

> Real learning comes about when the competitive spirit is ceased.
>
> —J. Krishnaurti

services, and the creation of more and better paying jobs. When there is less feeling of competition and more spirit of cooperation to find mutual solutions, there will be less need for looking out for Number One.

American society today experiences a most intense mixture of diverse cultures, customs, and practices. Multiculturalism requires the acceptance of the reality of our mutual interdependence and the need to lessen our exaggerated sense of individualism. Other-esteem mandates an immediate change of our perspective from a focus on self to one of consideration of others' feelings and concerns. It requires that we put away any sense of self or racial superiority over others and learn how to assimilate perspectives from different cultures into our daily lives with the same degree of esteem we expect for our own culture.

☐ The Balance of Self-Esteem and Other-Esteem

The functioning of self is very important to mental well being; however, this needs to be balanced with the acceptance and valuing of others in the same scale of mental wellness. We must learn, understand, and accept the self, not in a vacuum, but always in a complexity of relationship to others. The self is not whole without relationship with others.

Self-esteem and other-esteem are not mutually exclusive; they compliment each other and should be promoted simultaneously. Just as our lives—and thus our mental wellbeing and emotional equilibrium—are pervasively influenced and affected by people and events surrounding us, we also have an effect on others' thinking, feelings, and behavior. The only question is whether our effect on one another will be positive or negative.

☐ Examine Self and One's Cultural Background

The very first step in this esteem of others in our multicultural world starts with the knowledge of self. In order to fully understand and be able to accept others' cultures, we must tap into our inner selves and the cultural background in which we have grown up. The understanding of self, of one's values and beliefs, and of one's cultural background is of enormous help in understanding and valuing other cultures. This introspection of self may be long and painful, but meaningful insights can be attained that would be helpful in relating to other cultures.

Examine your own cultural background. It may include a variety or mixture of cultures. Look at the strengths and weaknesses of all facets of your cultural heritage. How do these values and beliefs make us feel, think, and behave differently from various ethnic groups within the society? Do we possess any biases or practice any prejudices towards any particular group or class or people? Does our cultural background have prevailing discriminations towards others? To what extent do we personally subscribe to these attitudes and behaviors? If we should discover any inconsistencies between what we believe and what we practice, we must then condemn our own stereotypes and generalizations. For example, do not laugh at ethnic jokes, as they perpetuate stereotyping.

Next, we must learn to accept and value some of our own beliefs and to challenge or reject those aspects of our cultural background, customs, and traditions that are in direct opposition to those beliefs. This process will help crystallize our values and strengthen our beliefs in ourselves and the culture in which we grew up. A truly self-assured person, one who accepts his or her culture, can better accept diversity and multiculturalism. By doing so, he attains a higher level of self-esteem, becomes more self-assured, and at the same time achieves a more exalted level of tolerance, acceptance, and valuing of others.

The next step is sharing one's cultural background and ideas. It is by sharing and inquiring of other's culture and customs that we come to know and understand each other better. A great deal of misunderstanding takes place in pre-conceived minds that cause us to value-judge others' behavior without taking a moment to inquire about their ideas, customs, or points of view. Be quick to inquire and slow to value-judge. Ask, teach, and learn are the three simple and basic, but necessary, keys to multicultural understanding.

I once heard this story about a Chinese student who flew 13 hours from Taipei to Los Angeles. Her non-Chinese professor met her at the airport and brought her home for a few days before school started.

The professor asked if she wanted any food or drink. In her typical oriental manner and expected reply, she said, "No." That night she went hungry. The lesson here is that the professor should have asked the student about the customary social exchanges in her country. The professor would have found out that an offer of food and drink to a Chinese guest is always politely declined. The host, however, should nevertheless bring the food and drink. Only then will the guest partake. Again, ask, teach, and learn. Do not take things for granted nor begin to accuse the other person of lack of sensitivity.

During a counseling convention, a female, Asian graduate student from California State University, who was about to make her presentation, requested her professor to move up front with her. The student presenter briefly stopped her speech and fetched a chair and offered it to her male Caucasian professor. The professor moved up front, took the seat, and sat down. What is the significance of the female Asian student's outward demonstration of respect for her male Caucasian professor? What can we all learn from this brief cultural encounter? Would Caucasian students act the same way toward their professors? How would an Asian professor react in similar circumstances?

☐ Respect Cultural Differences

Each of us is born into a certain culture and even into a more specific subculture. As we grow up, we interact and learn from those close to us and from society at large. We formulate our attitudes and become the way we are today. To paraphrase Albert Einstein's statement (quoted in Chapter 1) the problems we experienced today cannot be solved by the same level of

> The same necessity which secures the rights of person and property against the malignity of the magistrate determines the form and methods of governing, which are proper to each nation, and to its habit of thought, and nowise transferable to other states of society. In this country, we are vain of our political institutions . . . and we ostentatiously prefer them to any other in history. They are not better, but only fitter for us.
>
> —*Ralph Waldo Emerson*

consciousness that created them; we must learn to see the world anew. This re-learning can take place only from experience and from a completely different perspective. What are our personal encounters with people from different cultures? What have we internalized about people of color from books, newspapers, television programs, movies, and jokes? Which group do we have the least favorable impression of? Why? What generalizations, biases, and prejudices do we have towards various ethnic groups?

These questions are a starting point to cogitate seriously about respecting, accepting, and valuing others who may think, feel, and behave differently than you. At times, this need to esteem others who are different may be difficult or even unacceptable. At this point, are you able to approach the other person and share your feelings without condemning him? Listen to his or her explanation without any biased attitude or argumentative retort.

Multiculturalism in our society today should be beyond the point of sensitivity training or appreciation of ethnic dishes, songs, and dances. We should be at the stage of emotional maturity where one is able to communicate one's feelings without condemning or hurting another person. At the same time, we should be able to listen to the other person and try to understand the other person's point of view. This is other-esteem.

The American focus on the self and individual is in direct contrast to the focus on the family and society in Asian cultures. For example, foreign countries often comment that Americans are informal, spontaneous, laid back, and fun. We tend to communicate on a first name basis, often without regard to age differences, social position, or marital status. When we introduce each other, we usually refer to ourselves by our first names.

> Many of us seem to be stagnated in the oral stage. We talk too much and rarely listen. Too bad, Freud never wrote about an auditory stage.
>
> —Phil Hwang

However, most Asian cultures introduce individuals by giving the surname or family name first. In this way, people introduced can immediately relate others to their parents, siblings, and family. There is the realization of one's link to the family, and relationships are often based on a person's knowledge of another's relatives. These links are then the basis for future bonding.

Another example is the way we sign our names. Americans always begin with their first name and end up with their last name. The Chinese and many other Asian cultures put their last name or family name before their first name. What is the significance of these differences? Americans tend to focus on the individual, whereas Asians tend to focus on the family the individual comes from. American culture provides a greater degree of individuality and independence. Asian cultures frown on individuality and tend to promote family interdependence.

Most Asian cultures are group-oriented and group-dependent. Their cultures greatly dictate and direct the functioning of the individual within rather limited norms, customs and mores. The individual derives identity, self-esteem, and support from the country, family, colleagues, and friends. Group norms and traditions guide the individual's behavior within families, in relationships, and even within organizations.

There is a price for freedom and a price for social order. In Singapore, for example, public vandalism is punished by caning, a practice many Americans feel is a violation of human rights. But vandalism is rampant in the U.S. and insignificant in Singapore. In the United Kingdom, citizens are not allowed to have guns, which goes against the U.S. sentiment about the right to bear arms. But the rate of violent crime in the UK is significantly lower than that in the U.S.

Have our attitudes changed because for so long we worried about individual rights at the expense of social responsibility? There are no absolute personal human rights without related responsibility. Our demand for absolute individual freedom without our willingness to assume personal responsibility can only bring about chaos. If each of us were to assume responsibility for our own behavior, we would all be self-empowered. When we accuse others or blame circumstances for our misfortunes in life, then we acknowledge our destitution.

☐ Valuing and Accepting Others

A few years ago, while leading a group of psychiatrists, psychologists, and mental health professionals from the United States on a tour of China, I visited the Shanghai Psychiatric Hospital. In a roundtable discussion with some lay members of the hospital staff, many in our group were impressed with the hospital's release procedures. When patients are determined to be "safe enough" to return to society but are to continue treatment as outpatients, they are routinely assigned to a select committee. This committee is responsible for finding the person a job, making sure he continues to take the prescribed medication, and helping him to integrate back into society. Should the patient demonstrate any sign of deviance or disturbance, the committee notifies the hospital's doctors immediately. The committee, in consultation with the doctors, also makes the ultimate decision of returning the individual to the hospital for further diagnosis, treatment, or therapy.

In our society, however, mental patients who are ready for release are often set free into a dispassionate and uncaring society. Most former mental patients have a difficult time locating a job and are commonly discriminated against. Rarely will an individual with a history of mental illness be accepted back into society unless there are supportive family members and friends. Because such a support team is a rare commodity in our individualized society, mental relapses are common. Are we our brother's keeper? Should we care for others who need help?

Back in the 1950s, when France was ruling Vietnam, there were French schools. Vietnamese children enrolled in these elite schools were required to change their Vietnamese name to a French name. To this day, many of these children (now adults) hated what the French did to them, but they were too young to protest.

When the U.S. occupied the Philippines, Americans routinely imposed their public school system on that country. The Filipinos were taught only English. Students who dare to speak their native tongues were punished by school officials. Many of them grew up not knowing how to converse with each other in their own language.

These are but a few examples of lack of respect for and acceptance of others. When we are in a position to act, we should try to do the best we can to help others. We may very well need help ourselves one day. This is other-esteem for the less fortunate.

☐ Rights of the Majority

Just as minority groups possess rights in any given society, so does the majority have these same rights. We tend to think of our own rights and not so much of the rights of others. The first right of the majority is that they be given the benefit of the doubt. Every decision is not made on racial and ethnic issues. Our minds should remain open until there is absolute proof of discrimination.

Second, individuals should never use their minority status as a profession. One should not make a livelihood out of it. Being culturally different does not afford anyone privileges or benefits not available to everyone. Each of us must be as good as the best and better than the rest in both education and skills.

Third, not everyone in the majority group thinks and acts the same way. Negative attitudes and acts of discrimination are personal choices and individual decisions. It is not fair to generalize such behavior to an entire group. However, groups exist within our society where racial hatred and discrimination are the avowed goals in life. Their attitudes and behavior must be resisted and condemned by society and the world at large.

Finally, negative feedback towards an individual of color may be criticisms of specific behavior of that particular person who just happens to be a person of color. The criticisms may have absolutely nothing to do with an individual's minority identification. To generalize this personal inadequacy or failure to one's entire race is an individual defense mechanism. We refuse to see and discuss the issue at hand and instead attack the other person for racism. It is not only unjust to the other person, but we also perform a serious disservice to the minority group to which we belong.

All groups and sub-groups have the same rights as we do and should be respected by everyone else. Not every act is influenced by cultural differences, discriminations, prejudices, or biases. There are basic, universal, and fundamental principles governing human interactions. These inalienable human rights should be respected and adhered to by every citizen of the world and by every form of government. No single person, group of persons, or form of government has the right to abuse or discriminate against any particular individual or ethnic minority.

☐ The Majority Is Not Always Right

All decisions emanating from a position of power and/or majority status should be based on reasons and principles. However, in the words of Henry David Thoreau, ". . . the majority is not always right." There was a recent disturbing news report about an airline pilot who supposedly asked the passengers on a storm-threatened flight to raise their hands to vote on whether they would prefer to continue to New York City, or return to Chicago. A majority voted to continue on to New York. The pilot, unable to land in the storm at Kennedy Airport, put the plane down in a smaller airfield about an hour's drive from New York City.

If I had been on that plane, I would have been afraid of the consequences of allowing—even encouraging—an ignorant and aeronautically incompetent majority of passengers to make such a critical flight decision. In this case, a competent minority of ONE—the pilot—would have been sufficient to make the decision for every passenger, including me, on that plane. Although this flight ended safely, it is frightening to think that such a decision was put to an uneducated group for a vote where majority ruled.

Democratic principles of society are supposedly governed by the wishes of the majority. The simple principle "majority rules" seems a good enough process to make a decision, to choose a public official, and to run a government. "Majority rules," of course, assumes that people can freely express their opinions and agree on debated issues. Yet there are many times when this system is so abused by the ruling group that the opinions of the minorities are suppressed or ignored.

It is time for us to consider the possibility that the majority is NOT always right. A majority that does not listen to, does not have the information necessary to make intelligent decisions, or does not understand the feelings of the minority cannot effectively use the privilege of Majority Rule. Voting is an exercise in democratic principle only if all eligible voters are freely able and willing to cast their ballots.

Number and power do not automatically mean possession of wisdom and intelligence to make principled decisions! In fact, sometimes the opposite is true. Where number and strength exist, people may not feel it is necessary to exercise intelligence. Why bother to think and reason when intimidating the opposition is so easy? As we have seen in many countries, including the United States, this process is sometimes used to squash minority dissent, silence opposing groups, and rule by power and force.

History is fraught with evidence of the abuse of power and corruption by whichever political party is in power. As the majority, they have the strength and numbers to do whatever they wish. Nobody can stand in their way. In *The Human Factor* (1992), Graham Greene wrote: "Your worst enemies are not the ignorant and simple, however cruel; your worst enemies are the intelligent and corrupt."

Why rule on principle and reason when one can accomplish so much by power and might? This is reminiscent of the posse mentality and the lynch mobs of the wild west days. These groups claimed to be making decisions by the "voice of the people"—popular demand. But it does not take much research to learn that one or two self-righteous individuals, who may have had a personal grudge or might have benefited by the demise of the accused, could whip an audience into a lynching frenzy by emotion alone. In doing so, they bypassed the system of justice, based on logical and rational reasoning, set up to protect citizens and prevent acts of violence or retributions based purely on emotion and manipulation.

There is strong evidence that a similar situation exists today. The whipping-up of emotions with stirring rhetoric is a popular power tool. The only difference is that the power of the current majority comes from paper votes, whereas the lynch mobs used a sturdy rope. The questions we must ask are: Is the majority always right? Will the majority listen to reason and principle? Will it listen to one minority voice who teaches reason and principle, whose opinions deserve to be heard and evaluated? Sadly, the answer to all three questions is almost always "No." Thus, we need to be ever-vigilant in our

> It is the responsibility of the majority to seek out the opinion of the minority, just as it is the job of the extroverts to ask the introverts for their ideas.
> —*Phil Hwang*

criticism of the majority and never allow ourselves to fall into the trap of blindly following the majority without question.

In South Africa, the majority population had been ruled and denied voting rights by the powerful minority for many years. The powerful white minority ruled the country, utilizing the legal system to its advantage. They also controlled the economy through ownership and management of almost all trades and commerce. In early 1994, the country finally had a free election for all races. We should learn how to get rid of the distinction of majority-minority classification. Such classifications only lead to discrimination and biased attitude and behavior.

What are the alternatives to majority rule? One is consensus, in which group decisions are made such that everyone understands. In a consensus situation, not everyone in the group will necessarily agree with the decision that is made, but all agree that they can and will live with the outcomes.

☐ Diversity as a Choice and Not a Legal Mandate

Many organizations are reluctantly fulfilling employment quotas by hiring a certain percentage of minority employees.

> Develop consensus, because majority is not always right.
> —*Phil Hwang*

This supposedly "affirmative action" has often produced equal negative reaction from top management, colleagues, and others within a company. There are legal, moral, and ethical reasons to diversify. However, it is naive to think everybody agrees that multiculturalism is a desirable or a positive force for American society, and it is meaningful to do so only when it is embraced as a personal and organizational choice. It is not financially savvy for any organization to participate in a diversity program based purely on legal necessity. Such a program is doomed to failure. People will find excuses, loopholes, and blame for affirmative action programs when they are not convinced of the program's values.

> Gnossis Software is composed of . . . associates who possess great diversity economically, ethnically, and religiously. The diversity is a tremendous strength which contributes to all aspects of the company.
> —*Steve Kantor, President of Gnossos Software, Inc. and Foundation for Enterprise Development Business Leader of the Month, July 1999*

The important point to remember here is that multiculturalism must be embraced as a personal, corporate, and social choice and not as the fulfillment of a legal mandate. Deliberate choice and the acceptance of diversity are extremely positive forces for any organization. A diverse work force will eventually lead to more creative problem solving. People enriched with diversified backgrounds will approach decision-making processes differently. A multicultural-based company also can reach out to a broader clientele. In this way, the company's network is extended much further than a homogenous group. A multicultural work force will also enhance the productivity of the organization.

Those of us who believe in multiculturalism must strive to influence others who do not. We have a personal responsibility and moral obligation to sincerely promote and support multiculturalism. This is the only logical conclusion based on the principle of other-esteem. If we want others to esteem us, we must esteem others, no matter who they are.

We need to challenge and question the sincerity of organizations that take a dim view of diversity in their work force. These companies usually have devised a long list of excuses and rationalizations. The first objection they usually have is that qualified minority employees are difficult to find. The next excuse is that minority employees usually demand a higher salary. The third is that these employees will not fit into a company culture and that they will move on after a few years because other companies will recruit them.

These excuses are all defensive rationalizations. If a company does not want to change, it will come up with excuses. If we truly value a diverse work force and believe that it will greatly benefit **our** organization, we will find a way to recruit and retain a diverse group of employees.

Recruiting and retaining a culturally diverse work force for any organization is not an easy task. It takes determination and a firm commitment to the principles of multiculturalism. It also requires resources and strong support at all levels of the organization, especially from top management. Recruitment must be consistent and pro-active. We cannot just wait for vacancies and then advertise. Qualified, diverse candidates can be expected to walk in off the street without active recruitment and a demonstration that the workplace is friendly towards culturally diverse workers. Recruitment must be year-round and open-ended. When a qualified minority employee emerges, we should consider creating a position for her and not waiting until a vacancy exists. This is truly aggressive recruiting.

Retention is another issue. Many organizations fail in this important phase because young, talented employees are left to fend for themselves in a new, unfamiliar, and at times even unfriendly environment. There may be people within an organization who deliberately or subconsciously sabotage the attempt to recruit a multicultural work force in order to prove that people of color cannot succeed. This is more likely to happen among organizations and executives who are legally forced or pressured into hiring minority quotas. For this reason, decisions on minority hiring should be based on conviction and not on legal requirements.

The best way to make sure that prized recruits stay and become an asset to the organization is to request that an experienced senior staff member serve as a mentor. Programs and processes of mentoring include orientation, further education and training, and intensive networking that utilizes the mentor's experience, influence, and contacts. Along the way, there should be an appropriate level of challenging assignments. The objective here is not to be too protective but to provide proper guidance and counseling. Clearly defined goals and expectations should be set. The recruit should also have access to constant positive and constructive feedback and know exactly where she stands in the organization. The organization will soon benefit from its investment in multiculturalism when the employee becomes a positive force in the enterprises of the company.

☐ Networking and Promoting Multiculturalism

A network is a chain of helping hands linked together for mutual support and cooperation. One person alone cannot take on the entire cause of discrimination or the problems of organizational biases. You alone cannot right the wrong. Besides, your solution may not be the best method of solving the problem. As discussed in Chapter 6, we need to network with like-minded co-workers, colleagues, and trusted friends, and learn from and support each other's causes.

It is humbling to ask for others' help and support. But in the area of multiculturalism it is necessary. This is a very important reality check. Be part of a special group of dedicated, other-esteem oriented people who truly care and value each other. Get together and brainstorm on creative approaches to solving company problems.

The next step is to promote and celebrate multiculturalism within one's own organization and community. After decades of sensitivity training, we must forge ahead with action-oriented plans. Little can be gained by studying the different behaviors of various ethnic groups, unless that acquired knowledge is translated into perceivable behavioral changes that head to acceptance and respect for one another—the promoting of other-esteem.

If one promotes other-esteem of ethnic diversity and cultural pluralism, no race or culture is superior. One culture never puts down another. One race is never superior to another. There should not exist any quantitative competition or qualitative comparison. Every culture or race is different and unique in its own way. Each has its own history and chronicle of achievements and failures, of glorious accomplishments and of deplorable acts. Everyone is worthy of dignity, respect, love, and esteem. Where there are histories of conflicts, bloodshed, and hatred between two cultures or extremely complicated relationships among several groups of diverse backgrounds and ethnic origins, one needs to learn how to live for the future and not become stagnated in the past. This is the meaning of getting on with your own life.

> What have you done to promote multiculturalism in our society today ?
> —*Phil Hwang*

This is the ability to let go of an entangled past with a particular person or specific group of ethnicity. One cannot take on the causes of one's ancestors in order to continue historical enmity. Nor should one make others pay for the sins of the brothers, sisters, friends, and families. Today we live in a different time and in a completely transformed environment. We are all descendants of parties involved in ancient conflicts, discriminations, hatreds, abuses, and persecutions. Cultural and racial acceptance should start here and now, without carrying any further the burden of the tumultuous past. It is by this acceptance of the individual, completely unbiased and unburdened, that we can start building a more harmonious relationship.

Each day, ask yourself: "What have I done to promote multiculturalism today?"

☐ Key Concepts in This Chapter

1. Lack of other-esteem is the basis for discrimination.
2. Respect and accept others' cultural differences.
3. Examine one's own values and culture.
4. Develop a consensus, because majority is not always right.
5. Diversity is a choice and not a legal mandate.

The Psychology of Forgiveness

"The weak can never forgive. Forgiveness is the attribute of the strong."
—Mahatma Gandhi

Forgiveness is the ability to let go of an emotional hurt, to not be fettered by past painful experiences or consumed by plotting to get back at an oppressor, and to learn from an excruciating encounter and be ready to positively move on with one's life.

The ability and willingness to forgive someone is the height of other-esteem. It is easy to esteem others when they are prominent, successful, or considerate to us. But how about when they are unkind and rude, or have deliberately harmed us? How do we react to someone who has taken advantage of us and has brought us pain and suffering? Are we able to forgive? We can and we must! We must learn how to forgive for our own sake and to move on with our own lives.

This chapter contains theoretical views and specific principles on the psychology of forgiveness. These are important, generic overviews but in order for these concepts and suggestions to become meaningful, they must be personalized. Set aside all pre-conceived notions of forgiveness. Study these principles with an open mind. Read and discuss the thoughts and suggestions with someone you trust. Apply them to your personal situation and learn how to forgive, for healing is possible only through forgiveness.

☐ Pains and Forgiveness

Although forgiveness is a very common word, there are also many misconceptions about the psychology of forgiveness. I have been studying and exploring the issue of forgiveness for almost a decade. In that time, I have discovered that there is much pain in life. Everybody has a story to tell of undeserved pain and of bitterness for having been a victim.

> The ability and willingness to forgive someone is the height of other-esteem.
> —*Phil Hwang*

We can be shocked at the cruelty of supposed loved ones towards one another and dismayed at our level of insensitivity towards the feelings of others. Yet, if we become a victim, we all too often find ourselves scheming to get back at the perpetrator. We are not willing to let go until we obtain our "pound of flesh." Thus starts the personal cycle of neurosis, which can ultimately lead to a dysfunctional personality.

Forgiveness is the key to world peace and societal harmony. There is no greater need in the world today than the prerequisite of learning how to forgive, to let go of the past and to move on with life. What can we learn from the war between the Serbs and Croats in the former Yugoslavia Republic? What are the lessons from the killings of Catholics and Protestants in Northern Ireland? What are the causes of racial hatred and discrimination in our nation's communities? Most aspects of these conflicts are noted in past injustices and discriminations of one group against another. Retaliation generates retribution, and the cycle of violence continues. This neurotic cycle will only stop when one group decides to forgive another, and starts living for the future and not re-living past history.

Forgiveness is also the means to resolving many relationship conflicts involving race, gender, and family and work-related confrontations. The ability to forgive and the willingness to let go and move on can be a very liberating ingredient for living a life of mental wellness.

It is time to stop this vicious cycle. Practice other-esteem and no one will be abused. Those who have been hurt must learn how to forgive.

☐ Why Do We Not Forgive?

As human beings, none of us would be so bold as to claim that we are perfect and have never erred or hurt someone. If we are all less than perfect, does it not make sense that we would have greater tolerance for others' mistakes? It should not be so difficult to forgive the short-comings and grievous faults of those around us. However, one look at our fellow man is strong evidence that we are a most unforgiving species. We simply cannot or will not forgive others. Instead, we run the gamut from tongue-lashings to firearms, from gentle pokes to deadly beatings, all in the name of "teaching them a lesson."

This reaction is often influenced by cultural values and personal upbringing, and one's view of self versus others. The American culture's strong promotion of the self makes it difficult to forgive others. Many of these stumbling blocks to forgiveness are based on irrational fears and emotional reactions to painful life experiences.

Our society regards forgiveness as a weakness, an inability to stand up for oneself. We are well-schooled in the "John Wayne" toughness creed, the macho stance and the irrational eye-for-an-eye way of life. This teaches that a "man" does not forgive; he has to fight back. Such thinking makes it almost impossible for us to understand the need and rationale for forgiveness. But a glimpse into our history books will remind us of the many revered philosophers and renowned leaders who considered the ability to forgive to be more courageous and re-quiring greater strength than retaliation. It takes a truly magnani-mous person to say, "I forgive you." It is in this theoretical and prac-tical dichotomy of the most powerful of human emotions that we find ourselves torn apart, unable or unwilling to take the critical plunge.

Another reason for unwillingness or inability to forgive is the persis-tent fear that the offender may repeat the same act. We are afraid of being hurt again. We want to protect ourselves and break the cycle of pain, which is even deeper if the perpetrator is close to us and has shocked us by his unexpected actions. However, unwillingness to for-give does not guarantee that we will never be hurt again. There is no guarantee that if we do retaliate against the offender, he will have learned the lesson and the act will not be repeated. We must accept the fact that no matter what we do, we can never control external events or other people; we only have control over our own thoughts and actions. Thus, even though we may not be able to prevent the transgressors from hurting us again, we can prevent ourselves from becoming a victim forever by embracing the concepts of forgiveness. Keep in mind that the benefit of forgiveness is primarily for the victim and only incidentally for the perpetrator.

Some are unable to forgive society. James Oliver Huberty, a Viet-nam veteran, carried firearms into a McDonald's restaurant in San Ysidro, California, on a sunny July day in 1984. He launched a mind-less attack that killed 21 people and wounded 19 others before he was struck down by a SWAT team bullet. News reports said he was angry at society for "not treating him right." His unwillingness to forgive real and imaginary injustices must have contributed greatly to his actions on that fatal day.

Others are unable to forgive families and associates. On August 10, 1989, John Merlin Taylor shot and killed his wife, then drove to his work place at the post office in Escondido, California, where he killed two co-workers and wounded a third before putting the gun to his own head and pulling the trigger. News reports stated Taylor often blamed his wife for their financial problems and was experiencing increasing stress as a postal employee. His unwillingness to forgive others cost four people their lives and untold sufferings for their families.

Others cannot forgive themselves. How many of us go over and over in our heads the mistakes we make long after the situations or circumstances are gone and others have forgotten them? Holding on to mistakes does not free us to live in the present and to move on to the future; it keeps us rooted in the past.

The effects of unforgiveness are clear: a bitter and unproductive life for both the victim and the persecutor. Unforgiveness ensures that we will live surrounded by unforgivable events that prevent us from living in the here and now of reality; our preoccupation with the past will cause untold mental and physical stress, and we will discover that absorption with revenge clouds our minds against positive and productive pursuits. In other words, our unwillingness to forgive others prevents us from living up to our full potential. Instead of "letting go" of the painful past, beginning to live in the present, and starting to looking forward to future endeavors, our preoccupation with past miseries, pains, and hurts will stagnate our minds and curb our zest for life.

☐ Six Basic Principles of Forgiveness

There is a need to transcend the emotionality of the issue of forgiveness and to narrow its focus. We cannot take on the entire world to redress our wrongs, nor can we bring back past events of life. All study on forgiveness must be deliberated in its total complexity with only one goal: focusing on the future well-being of the victim. The following "Principles of Forgiveness" are written with this in mind.

1. Forgiveness Is Necessary to Our Mental Well Being

Conveniently, we have relegated forgiveness to the realm of religion and writings of theologians. Forgiveness may have religious significance, but it is also a fundamental concept within the daily activities of human interaction. We owe it to ourselves to look at forgiveness from the standpoint of mental health rather than religious command-ments. Our religious preferences are as varied as the birds in the sky, but we all have the same need for secure mental health.

Forgiveness is a prelude to personal peace of mind, charged like a heavenly miracle with powerful healing energy. We are all familiar with the expression, "to err is human; to forgive, divine." However, forgiveness is not just a divine attribute, but a human necessity for a happy and healthy balance in our lives.

Once we are able to forgive someone for a transgression against us—whether real or imaginary—we immediately discharge a heavy burden from our minds. Tensions stored deep within begin to relax and release, wiping out the unpleasant experience and moving us closer to closure of that unpleasant chapter of our life.

Without this cleansing forgiveness, our minds will cook and boil all the different negative ingredients with every recollection of the un-pleasant past experience. Before we know it, we are concocting vi-cious schemes to get even or harm the other party in some way. Our revengeful mind nags, "Teach them a lesson so they won't mess around with me anymore."

There is a direct correlation between forgiveness and revenge. The primary and instinctive human emotion holding us back from for-giving someone is our instinctive gut reaction of retaliation against someone who has hurt us. Many of us actually live by the slogan, "Don't get mad, get even!" We want to hurt the other person so badly, even if it means our total destruction too.

The fact that revenge is instinctive, natural, and humanly understand-able does not make this destructive emotion acceptable or helpful to our well-being. Human beings did not come to dominate the world by reacting on gut instinct or acting on emotional desires; we came to dominate the world because our species can think and reason.

Forgiveness means that even though a person has hurt us miser-ably, we will not seek revenge by inventing creative tortures to hurt the person back. Our refusal to seek revenge does not signify that we approve or condone the action, but rather it is an acceptance that enough pain has already been caused. By telling the perpetrator, firmly and with conviction, that we have no intention of committing the same pain, we are sending the message that we will not make the same mistake as that person did and we will not allow this hurtful action to mar our peace of mind. By choosing to forgive, we are also notifying the transgressor that he has no power over us and that no matter what, we have decided to move on with our life.

Memories are like computers. If they are programmed to store hurtful experiences, those hurts can be recalled at a moment's notice. One can even try to convince oneself that vengeful behavior will release pent-up anger and tension, but that is playing a fool's game. The input and storage of vengeful thoughts and emotions within the mind create extremely negative energies that are detrimental to your physical and mental health and to the health of those around you. Forgiving and giving up anger can have a powerful influence to heal physical ailments, including the reversal of heart disease (Ornish, 1998).

We must remember that nobody is perfect, least of all ourselves. Think of all the mistakes we have made in our lives. Did other people condemn us because of our mistakes? Or were we given a second (or third) chance? Think back on our relationship with our parents. How often were we forgiven by them for misbehaviors ranging from trivial incidents to more serious offenses with the words, "Oh, they really don't mean it," or "They are still young!" A rationalization to be sure—but such rationalization makes it easier to forgive someone.

We may not have been aware of it, but throughout our lives, we have been forgiven many times for our transgressions, and we, in turn, have forgiven others for theirs. An action that causes pain is usually not directed at the victim, but is the result of self-centered ego satisfaction behavior. In the past, our acts of forgiveness may have been based on instinct and emotion (i.e., love for our children and family). Now, we must take this one step further and make a deliberate choice to forgive others, not just because we love them, but because of the beneficial aspects to our own mental health.

Unforgiveness, on the other hand, turns us into victims forever. We relive the pain and hurt over and over again, programming ourselves so deeply that the most remote hint—a book title, a word from a stranger, a song on the radio, a flashing billboard, a whiff of perfume—reminds us of our shackles of bitter memories. Our inability to forgive will increase our burden of internal pain and suffering with each passing day. This chain of agony can only be broken by forgiving and forgetting. Otherwise, we will stagnate in our own bitter memories of hurt

> Forgiveness is primarily for our own sake, so that we no longer carry the burden of resentment.
>
> —*Buddha*

and pain, unable to go on with our lives. Our refusal to let go will only cause unhappiness and stress to ourselves, those we love, and everyone around us.

2. Forgiveness Is a State of Mind, a Conviction of Attitude

Forgiveness is a deliberate choice of our mind, not just words or feelings. In our society, too much emphasis has been placed on "emotions" and "feelings." Not nearly enough attention has been placed on cognition, which is the most important part of the human process because it influences attitudes, affects our emotions, and dictates our subsequent behavior. After all, human emotion is truly the product of the mind. The first step in experiencing a happy event is the actual and deliberate interpretation of selected stimulus; positive emotions will then naturally flow directly from it.

Furthermore, the change of attitude from revenge to forgiveness is not a single act. It is one of the few human emotions that demands repetition. The greater the hurt, the greater the need for repeated forgiveness—and the more time and effort it will take to achieve it. One deliberate act of the mind to forgive someone for an injustice may be enough to soothe the immediate pain and suffering of the moment, but if the hurt is deep and personal, repeated acts of forgiveness are necessary.

Forgiveness signifies a deliberate choice, a letting go of the pain and hurt, and the beginning of the healing process. A woman who was badly injured in a drunk driving accident went to court in her wheelchair and petitioned the judge not to give prison time to the drunk driver but instead to send him to rehabilitation. This was the ultimate in forgiveness. Sending the drunk driver to prison would not bring back her physical health, but re-education might change his life. The woman made the choice to forgive and, in doing so, began her own emotional healing.

3. Forgiveness Is for the Sake of the Forgiver, Not the Forgiven

The major principle in the psychology of forgiveness is that forgiveness offers more benefits to the forgiver than to the forgiven. Acts of torment are in the past, but pains and sufferings are experienced today. Victims can become survivors only through forgiveness. The deeper the hurt, the more urgent the need for forgiveness.

Lena was angry at Bo for leaving her to marry someone half her age. For two years she lived a bitter life and constantly thought of ways to get back at her ex-husband. Friends suggested that she go into therapy. After two months of intensive group counseling, Lena wrote her ex-husband a short note of forgiveness. Her whole life changed. She is re-married and very happy in her career.

Lena's forgiveness of her ex-husband freed her from being a victim forever. Bo's hold on Lena stopped the very moment Lena chose to let go of her past. She had a new view of life and was able to move on.

> To forgive does not mean we will allow injustice again.
> —*Buddha*

Forgiveness Does Not Mean Condoning Behavior

By forgiving, we neither condone nor tolerate a wrong, mean-spirited, or hurtful event. We are not encouraging the recurrence of the painful experience, and we can demand that something be done to ensure that it will not be repeated. These painful events must be brought out in the open, so that reconciliation can take place and help provided for all involved.

Forgiveness is not "turning the other cheek" and letting the action be repeated; on the contrary, forgiveness means learning from the experience and taking rational and fair means to prevent a recurrence. Forgiveness involves condemning the act, not the actor. Thus, we speak out, but we do not shout. We counsel, but we do not condemn the person we are forgiving. We demonstrate alternatives and do not block out individual chosen paths to wellness.

4. Forgiveness Applies to Minor Irritations as Well as Great Injustices

Many of us think that forgiveness refers only to the great injustices of life, as though, unless there is huge trauma such as financial deception, sexual molestation, or betrayal of trust, there is nothing to forgive. We do not have to go around every day saying, "I forgive you, I forgive you," to all minor human insensitivities; however, we do need to let go of all those irritations. Do not store all these pains and hurts or they may overload until at some point you reach your proverbial "last straw" and explode.

American society tends to be an unforgiving society, quick to condemn the behavior of others. In the blink of an eye we appoint ourselves prosecutor, judge, and executioner of those around us. We blame others and want to make them pay for all kinds of wrongdoings, real or imagined, large or small.

I witnessed an example of this recently when I was stopped at a red light on a busy Los Angeles intersection. Across the street, coming towards me, was a small compact car racing to beat the just-turned-red traffic light. The driver of a rusty sedan on my left deliberately jumped his green light and smashed into the side of the "offending" car. He then leapt out of his sedan, ran over to the dazed driver of the damaged vehicle and screamed loudly, "This will teach you not to run red lights!" Somewhere in this crazed man's mind must have flashed the words, "That's the last straw." He then followed with a barrage of outrageous condemnation.

How many straws did it take to reach this man's limit? How many does it take to reach yours? Think for a moment about the load of straws you are hauling around right now. Do these straws justify a tirade of irrational behavior resulting in hurt to other people's emotional or physical well-being or damage to property?

Too many people are walking around like time bombs because they have consciously or unconsciously accumulated explosive emotions of "getting even." These people are teetering on the brink of disaster; it does not take much to ignite these time bombs.

Every day we are shocked by news reports of such incidents, and sociologists and psychologists are often at a loss to explain such behaviors. The only psychological cure learning the willingness to "let go" and the determination to forgive.

Do not let the load of straws build up by being unable or unwilling to forgive others. With forgiving and learning to interpret life events differently comes a letting go of the "straws" we ordinarily haul around. As we let go of more straws, the chances of our ever reaching the last one decreases. With fewer straws to burden our psyche, we can improve our mental well-being and live a happier life. By opening our eyes to the wonderful power and magic of forgiveness, we can sweep aside each straw as it comes.

5. Forgiveness Is a Personal Choice—
Not a Religious Obligation

Forgiveness is a gift. As a gift, it can only be freely given by the deliberate choice and generosity of the giver. Forgiveness cannot be demanded by the recipient or commanded by religious mandates. Forgiveness cannot be earned or demanded by threats. Forgiveness is a gift, based on the personal choice and the individual desire to "let go" and to "get on."

Realizing that forgiveness is our choice, we understand that by forgiving others, we are taking other esteem into account in two ways. On one hand, we cannot demand or earn forgiveness from others, so in other-esteem thinking, we must apologize for our wrong-doings, then let go and not try to coerce another into forgiving us. And, on the other hand, when we are the one in the position to forgive, it is important to know that it IS our choice and we forgive not because we have to, but because it is the wise choice. Other-esteem thinking would have us forgive others both for our own sake and theirs and for the sake of the relationship. Making the wise and informed choice keeps us from having the resentment we might have if we thought we HAD to forgive.

6. Unforgiveness Is Destructive—
Forgiveness Is Constructive

From reading newspapers or watching news on TV, we all know how destructive unforgiveness can be. Below are a few examples of extremely unforgiving behaviors exhibited by people who reached their "last straw." How many examples come to your mind as you read these samples?

- In a restaurant, a patron who was smoking in a non-smoking section was requested by a non-smoking customer to put out his cigarette. He did and walked out of the establishment. A few minutes later he came back with a gun and shot the complaining patron to death.
- A high school student was beaten to death by a gang of other students because he unknowingly was wearing a jacket with a color that belonged to the rival gang.
- Two cars pulled into a parking lot from different directions at about the same time. Both drivers noticed the only space available. The driver of the smaller car was able to squeeze his car into the space. Furious, the driver of the second car got out of his vehicle and scratched the side of the parked car with a key.

Forgiveness is the conversion of negative attitudes, feelings, and behaviors into positive and productive forces for self, family, and society. Forgiveness can be compared to the construction of new bridges after a disastrous earthquake. After the initial shock, the subsequent pain and suffering take a heavy toll in both emotional strain and physical dysfunction. In a personal sense, the human bridge of our relationship has collapsed in a rubble. It is now time for rebuilding: this is forgiveness.

☐ **Three Phases of Forgiveness**

Forgiveness, like so many emotional and psychological aspects of our lives, moves through different phases of experiencing and reacting. These phases are not distinct and sequential stages, like Freud's theory of psycho-sexual development. Experiencing hurt and our reaction to it is a very personal and unique one. The length of recovery can also vary from few moments to years of struggle and continued positive affirmation.

In dealing with forgiveness, one often can identify a Painful Phase, a Destructive Phase, and a Healing Phase. Within each phase are stages and/or identifiable roles played either by the victim or the perpetrator. The perpetrator is not necessarily a specific person or persons. It could be an event or coincidence of happenings.

It is the perceived hurt experienced by the victim that is of greatest concern to us. The focus is on the hurt experienced, the subsequent reaction to it and, finally, the victim's decision about the future.

1. The Painful Phase of Forgiveness
(The Victim Experiences the Pain)

Stages	Victim's Reactions
Initial encounter	Shock and disbelief
Period of exploration	Search and question
Period of reckoning	Condemnation

Initial Encounter

The first phase of forgiveness is the Painful Phase. The Painful Phase begins with the initial experience or realization of a hurtful feeling from an individual or event. Quite often, this first encounter takes place accidentally. It may be a chance happening of unlikely related events, a slip of the tongue, or a discovery of information that could hit one like a storm and shake up all the senses.

During this period, victims realize they are experiencing pain they feel they do not deserve. The source of this pain may be injustice within the society or wanton callousness from a friend or a loved one. It does not matter. There is a sad story to share that may be painful to even think or talk about it. What they do know is that they are hurting.

This phase is characterized by confusion, disbelief and helplessness. The victims do not know what to say or whom to believe. The impact of this unexpected intrusion into life's equilibrium destroys their semblance of fragile balance and creates contradictory feelings of anger and helplessness.

They are angry because they are hurt, perhaps by someone whom they trusted or thought loved them. Such is the effect of incest, the betrayal of a spouse, and the deceptive lies of business associates. They feel simultaneously helpless and seemly devoid of physical strength or emotional response. They are dazed, as if zapped by an invisible and invincible force beyond any describable proportion.

Period of Exploration

After the initial stage of confusion, chaos, shock, and disbelief, victims often become wild and confused and wander aimlessly both emotionally and physically. They may begin a desperate and frantic search to discredit and even to challenge the veracity of the hurtful incident. These victims will try to rationalize and minimize the evil intention of the persecutor.

Failing this futile effort, they will then switch to a frantic search for the ugly and painful details of who, what, where, when, and how from anywhere and anyone, including the perpetrator. Victims are usually governed by a high level of mistrust, and yet are pre-occupied with an almost detective-like fervor in an attempt to seek clues to understand the painful situation. This often includes a lot of hearsay, rumors, and exaggerations, which more than likely will enlarge the depth and breadth of the wound.

Soon the victims are spinning in a neurotic circle: the more they search, the more confused they become. The more confused they are, the deeper the hurt and anger. There seems to be no bottom to this painful experience, and no rational or logical explanation for what has just taken place. As the picture of events becomes muddier, the ability to comprehend and understand decreases further.

Period of Reckoning

As soon as victims accumulate snippets of information, whether real, imaginary, or concocted, they confront the offender and angrily demand answers and explanations. They now play the roles of the police, prosecuting attorney, the judge, and even the jury. The verdict: guilty!

At this point, no matter how remorseful or honest the offender's account of actual events, a web of justifications or excuses will seldom satisfy the victim's insistence of the perpetrator's absolute guilt. At times, the extent of the hurt and perhaps event the degree of guilt is exaggerated beyond reality as the victim mixes limited facts with wild fantasies of the mind.

This phase is marked by violent confrontations, often in the form of seemingly endless arguments, repetitive emotional outbursts, and incessant nasty fights. No satisfaction can be found for either party. This volatile period is often short in duration. However, the struggle may be protracted, especially if it involves couples who live together, for no two people can live under the same roof in such an emotionally charged and aroused state of constant bickering, absolute mistrust, and hurt. Victims will soon realize the uselessness of digging out the dirty details; perpetrators either blame or rationalize their errors, or decide that their behavior was indefensible and that no explanation will ever justify their actions.

2. The Destructive Phase of Forgiveness (The Victim Reacts to the Past)

Stages	Victim's Message
Role of victim	Pity me
Role of avenger	Get even

The destructive phase follows almost immediately. This phase can be described as the victims' reaction to the Painful Phase. During this time, victims can react in at least two different ways: in the role of Victims, or in the role of Avengers. They may also vacillate between these two roles, depending on circumstances and the benefits obtained from these reactions. These are both very powerful and yet destructive behaviors and are not mutually exclusive.

Human behaviors are purposeful. There is purpose behind each of our behaviors. This purpose may be deliberate or unconscious. Thus, playing the role of being an abused person or an avenger has payoffs.

Role of the Victim

Almost immediately after the Painful Phase comes a period of despair and hopelessness. This highly charged period is characterized by victims' withdrawal into self-pity, into a hole of ever-constant, self-defeating, depressing thoughts. During this time, victims relive, and often even re-create and mentally exaggerate, the hurtful event just experienced.

This self-pity is a very natural and human reaction to the immediacy of the experience. At this point, all negative feelings and ridiculous behaviors are justified in the minds of the victims by what has happened. Some of the negative and destructive messages of victimhood are:

- "I have been hurt. I am a helpless victim."
- "Surely you don't expect me to live a normal life. Can't you see what has happened to me?"
- "See what you have done to me? It's all your fault!"
- "All is lost. I have no reason to live."
- "Have pity on me! Surely you must feel sorry for me."
- "Nobody really loves me and cares about me. Why should I live on?"

You can probably think of many other defeatist statements. How often have we reacted and chosen to play the role of the victim? The role of the victim is perhaps the most painful and difficult of all the phases, because the victim has the tendency to withdraw from life and normal activities. The only meaningful feeling for the victim at this point is the painful experience. Life no longer seems to have any meaning or purpose. A "poor me" attitude prevails, darkening all normal perception in relationships with family, friends, and colleagues. Indeed, to the victim, the world suddenly looks as drab and bleak as the moonscape. It is a cold and cruel world out there.

The role of the victim is a powerful one, and it can be rewarding at times. It communicates to the perpetrators the degree of pain and hurt caused by their actions and is meant to increase his guilty feelings as a way of getting back at them.

Victims also attract attention and sympathy from everyone who is aware of the injustices inflicted. People often come to the aid of the victims. Knowing when to play the victim role and at what precise moment, the victim could regain certain semblance of control and power. The problem with such an action is that this unknowingly reinforces a negative and destructive behavior. As long as victims are rewarded for their "poor me" or "have pity on me" behaviors, they will never move to a more constructive set of behaviors.

There are people who play the role of the victim so successfully that their plights become their profession. They profit from telling their tales to anyone or any organization willing to pay.

The role of the "The Victim" is a destructive behavior because it is manipulative and a form of passive-aggressive behavior. No positive outcome will be derived from such a behavior.

Role of the Avenger

After wallowing for a time in despair and mourning, victims begin to harbor thoughts of revenge, to right the wrong. The victim's mind constantly repeats a discordant melody: "This will only make sense to me if I retaliate. What can I do to hurt them as deeply as I have been hurt? How dare they do this to me! I'll show them!"

This period is often long and extremely ugly, charged with bitterness and frequently leading to disastrous and tragic consequences. The role of avengers here is to inflict pain on the perpetrators as much and in as many ways as possible. They want to get even with the perpetrators to prevent such an occurrence from happening again.

- Joseph was furious when his neighbors complained about the trees in his yard being too high and obstructing their view. He was asked to cut the trees down to size. He did. The one night, just to get even, Joseph poisoned his neighbors' fruit trees.
- Jim has not called his father "Dad," for at least ten years. Instead, he calls him by his first name, John, because Jim despises his father for being an alcoholic and bringing so much pain and suffering to the family. This is Jim's way of getting back at his father.

Revenge comes in different forms. Victims are very creative when they want to get even with or hurt others. They do so in a variety of ways, including:

- Threats or actual acts of physical violence
- Verbal abuses of criticism, rumors, and damaging remarks
- Destruction of perpetrator's property or business
- Creation of numerous little irritations and nasty annoyances,
- Withholding of love and emotional supports

Many victims stagnate in the revenge stage and never come to know the healing process. Some put such traumatic finality to their painful experiences that they turn their tormentors into victims, and in the process sometimes take along innocent bystanders. Still others take the path of

> Absorption with revenge clouds our minds against positive and productive pursuits.
> —*Phil Hwang*

becoming a psychological tormentor by constantly taking pot-shots at the perpetrator and/or refusing to accept his or her apology. The daily media is full of news stories that report the multitude of individuals making the choice to rot their minds and emotions in this disastrous revengeful role.

3. The Healing Phase of Forgiveness (The Victim Chooses)

Stages	Victim's Behavior
Acceptance	Facts of life you can't change
Reconciliation	Condemn the act and not the person
Moving On	Live for tomorrow
New Life	New person and distinct goals in life

The Healing Phase is a giant leap forward from the destructive phase. True forgiveness begins at this point. The earlier phases describe the experiences and reactions of a hurt individual. Now comes the period of decision: victims must decide whether they want to get out of the destructive phase and into the healing phase. Once the decision is made, the stages of this phase come in rapid succession.

This period of re-building takes a great deal of time and patience, and is often characterized by a roller-coaster of emotional ambiguity, indecision, and painful internal conflicts. This decision needs to be arrived at from within and cannot be dictated from without or by any other external force. Thus, decisions regarding future personal inter-action are continually punctuated by vacillation and self-doubt.

A very important characteristic of this phase is that it is often inter-rupted with frequent relapses. Taking the first step towards forgiveness and into the healing process is sometimes scary and very tentative. Any negative reaction or averse reinforcement can cause the victim to with-draw once again into one of the many roles in the destructive phase, particularly if the offender continues to perpetuate the same behavior. It is also a "recycling" phenomenon, characterized by a process of two steps forward and one step backward. Progress is very slow and can be quite painful, but progress is attainable for those who are determined to succeed.

Acceptance

This is the true beginning of the healing process. Victims have had enough of the destructive behaviors exhibited by both themselves and the perpetrators. None of the roles played during the hurtful phase produced any positive results, so victims are now willing to accept the following facts of life:

- Someone has caused them pain they did not deserve.
- There is nothing they can do now or in the future to delete this event from their lives.
- They alone can bring back their own peace of mind.

Reconciliation

Just as the self is incomplete without the other, healing cannot be complete without some kind of reconciliation with the perpetrator. This reconciliation may actually take place with a face-to-face meeting, over the phone, or even through a short note of forgiveness.

The ability to reconcile makes forgiveness more meaningful and complete. However, although the perpetrator will benefit greatly from it, reconciliation is still for the benefit of the forgiver. Many are unwilling to reconcile for fear of looking weak or fear that the perpetrator will hurt them again. These fears are legitimate and, for these reasons, it is easier to forgive a stranger than a loved one. However, forgiveness does not always mean returning to the "good old days" (which may not have been good to begin with).

Forgiveness does not always mean togetherness again. Although in forgiveness there is a condemnation of the act and not the actor, and victims want to let perpetrators know about the forgiveness, it is also important for the perpetrator to know that the hurt will not be tolerated in the future. The victims will be out of harm's way. In some cases, that means there will no longer be a relationship with that person.

Moving On

Once victims make the decision to accept the reality of the situation and reconcile with the past experience of hurt, their next step is to get on with life. Moving on also means being liberated from the roles they thought they had to play. The stage of "moving on" has the following characteristics for victims:

- No longer dwelling on the past
- Starting to plan for the future
- Strategizing about the alternative lifestyle without the hurt or victim roles
- Starting to make life changes
- Feeling all right about themselves

New Life

Every life experience, both negative and positive, affords an opportunity for learning. The Chinese language translates the word "crisis" into two words: "danger" and "opportunity." The experience that may have caused the hurt represents the danger, and the healing process that can lead to a new learning that benefits both those involved and others is the opportunity. Because of what they experienced and learned from their pain, victims can now empathize better with others who have had similar experiences. They can become part of others' support networks. They can reach out to others who, just as they once were, may be in pain, some still stagnated in the destructive phase. The question now is how to support others in their decision to move on to the healing phase.

A couple whose teenage son was killed by a drunk driver generously volunteered their time and money to Mother Against Drunk Driving (MADD).

Parents whose daughter was kidnapped, sexually abused, and then murdered now dedicate their life to helping other parents look for their missing children.

A deeper understanding of the concept of forgiveness should encourage us to take a hard look at our current relationships and the way we deal with difficult events in our lives (see Figures 8.1, 8.2, and 8.3). Be honest with yourself: are you a person who is unable to forgive society, those around you, or even yourself? Are you someone who loves to "stir up the pot" just to watch others writhe and squirm in agony? Perhaps you harbor grudges, relish confrontation, or love to wallow in self-pity? Regardless of your past disposition, forgiveness can lift a crushing burden from your shoulders and introduce you to a personal peace you never before thought possible.

☐ Key Concepts in This Chapter

1. Forgiveness is the height of self-esteem and other-esteem.
2. Revenge is harmful to our mental health.
3. Forgiveness sets us free and reclaims our peace of mind.
4. Six Basic Principles of Forgiveness are:

   - Forgiveness is necessary to our mental well-being.
   - Forgiveness is a constant state-of-mind, a conviction of attitude.
   - Forgiveness is for the sake of the forgiver and not the perpetrator.

- Forgiveness applies to minor irritations as well as great injustices.
- Forgiveness is a personal choice, not a religious obligation.
- Unforgiveness is destructive; forgiveness is constructive.

5. The three phases of forgiveness are: Painful Phase, Destructive Phase, and Healing Phase.

---

1. Painful Phase of Forgiveness (You experience the hurt)

Stages	Victim's Reactions
Initial encounter	Shock and disbelief
Period of exploration	Search and question
Period of reckoning	Condemnation

2. Destructive Phase of Forgiveness (You react to the past)

Stages	Victim's Message
Role of victim	Pity me
Role of avenger	Get even

3. Healing Phase of Forgiveness (You choose)

Stages	Victim's Behavior
Acceptance	Facts of life you can't change
Reconciliation	Condemn the act and not the person
Moving On	Live for tomorrow
New Life	New person with distinct goals in life

FIGURE 8.1. Three phases of forgiveness.

A. Jot down when and how certain people/events have hurt you.
(FEELING-THINKING-ACTION)

1. _____

2. _____

3. _____

B. Identify solutions or ways to rid the above hurt you don't deserve.

1. _____

2. _____

3. _____

FIGURE 8.2. Forgiveness is ridding yourself of hurt you don't deserve.

Write honestly and unselfconsciously for a few minutes as you visualize yourself in the particular situations. Say loudly in your mind: "Today, for my own mental sanity, I choose to forgive because I want to MOVE ON."

A. I forgive MYSELF for: _____
_____
_____
_____

B. I forgive OTHERS (be specific) for: _____
_____
_____
_____

C. I forgive SOCIETY for: _____
_____
_____
_____

_____   _____
Signature   Date

FIGURE 8.3. Forgiveness.

The By-Ways to a Meaningful Life

"Two roads converged in a wood and I took the one less traveled by, and that has made all the difference."

—Robert Frost

Our journey through life takes place on a road filled with twists and turns, challenges, and the need for constant decisions. When we arrive at critical junctions, we are forced to make choices. Sometimes, we must make split-second decisions; at other junctions, we have the luxury of time to explore a myriad of alternatives before choosing what is meaningful for us and what is good for others in a more and more diverse society.

Many experts of our society have talked about successes in life, acquisition of wealth, becoming skillful leaders, etc. What we need are more people to discuss the meaningfulness of life and ways to live by it.

As we have explored in earlier chapters, our attitudes, values, and experiences influence our decisions. We may also be deeply affected by what our family and friends expect of us. But as a society, we have been unwilling to stand up for our values and maintain a balance between personal rights and social responsibilities.

The sole purpose of this book has been to convert your emphasis from self to a healthy balance of self- and other-esteem, living a meaningful life in a multicultural society. The decision to live a life of other-esteem is, at the present time in our multicultural society, the "road less traveled by," and is by no means generally accepted. Achieving this balance will take time, effort, and deliberate training. This final chapter explores the ways in which we can view life differently and focuses on alternative responses to life decisions we face every day.

> Happiness is a state of mind. It is always available at a bargain price.
> —*Ancient Chinese Proverb*

It takes courage to be different, to deviate from the comfort and security of the expected. But consider the rewards. By knowing what is right for you and adhering to your chosen values and principles, you will be able to see beyond the daily routine to focus on larger, more meaningful issues. Achieving the balance of self- and other-esteem will result in a more creative and innovative lifestyle, and life will seem more interesting and fulfilling.

The question is: which path do you want to take in life? Do you have the courage to take the less trodden path, the by-way to meaningful life, to risk being different for the benefit of others and yourself? What is the way or the by-way to follow to reach your ultimate goal of meaningful life?

☐ Personal Wellness Training Program

Professional athletes train long hours for months and years to get into top physical shape. They lift weights, jog, and maintain a rigid program of balanced nutrition and diet. They also train with other athletes and perfect their skills together. They do all of this to achieve their dreams of meeting their highest potential.

But human beings do not go through any training program for the personal and psychological events of life. There is no training program to prepare us to deal with daily personal stresses. Positive and negative experiences and our reactions to them are very much left to chance. No wonder the world is full of walking wounded with emotional scars and psychological traumas.

We worry more about our physical conditioning and appearance than about the acquisition of emotional strength and psychological know-how needed to deal with the ups and downs of daily of life. This needs to change immediately. Each one of us must prescribe a personal wellness program for ourselves, set a definite schedule of practice and attainment, solicit support *from* others, and offer your support *for* others' journeys through the by-ways of life.

☐ Your Roadmap: The Wheel of Meaningful Life

The by-ways to meaningful life simply cannot be traveled alone. We all need companions along the way. The route we take is not a straight shot, but a winding road that entwines our lives inseparably with the lives of others. Both self- and other-esteem are necessary to finding true happiness as we discover the connection and flow between caring for ourselves and caring for others. The Wheel of Meaningful Life (see Figure 9.1) is a model incorporating six elements that connect to bring about a balanced, happy and meaningful life:

- The By-Way to Knowledge of Self and Others
- The By-Way to Nurturing Self and Others

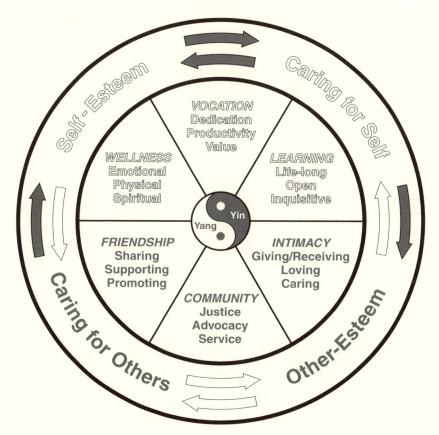

FIGURE 9.1. Wheel of meaningful life.

- The By-Way to Inner Peace and Harmony with Others
- The By-Way to Life of Interdependency
- The By-Way to Friendship and Fellowship
- The By-Way to Leadership and "Followship"

This chapter is your personal training program as you go along the by-ways. You will see specific suggestions in each area—suggested building blocks for your by-ways to meaningful life. They are meant to start you but you must pick and choose and personalize and re-shape the building blocks to pave your own by-ways of life.

1. The By-Way to Knowledge and Acceptance of Self and Others

Your Uniqueness

Most of us sell ourselves short. We are all unique and precious. By developing and promoting that uniqueness and knowing that each of us brings to life our own individual and special skills, talents, and gifts that can be shared with others, we are all free to contribute to abetter life for everyone. Your contribution is necessary and important. Honor your uniqueness and promote and value the uniqueness of others.

Vocation: A Mission in Life

"He who knows himself is a wise person." This famous ancient saying of the Chinese philosopher Zhuang Zi has often been quoted. How many wise and intelligent people know a multitude of facts and theories, but do not have an inkling about who they are inside or how their behaviors have affected others?

How many people have examined their own motivations, feelings, purposes, goals, ideals, and chosen principles? How can we consider ourselves educated if we know nothing about the only person we can ever truly know—ourselves? Wise and educated persons know what motivates them and what makes them happy. They know about their strengths and weaknesses, and about what works within that framework of knowledge.

> The life, which is not examined, is not worth living.
> —*Plato*

Discovering who we are, who we want to be, and where it is best for us to go will give us an awareness of our individual strengths and limitations and encourage us to seek the most appropriate path. This is what it means to find our vocation.

Think about your daily behavior over the past few months or years. At the same time, seek feedback, both positive and negative, from people who care about your tranquillity and happiness in life. What factors have shaped your outlook on life and what has motivated you? There is an important distinction between external and internal motivating factors. People who are motivated by internal rewards see and approach life from a much different perspective than people who are motivated by external rewards. External rewards include money, success, power, influence, fame, and the ability to acquire material things. Internal rewards are not materialistic in nature and can be as simple as the feeling of satisfaction we get when we help someone or put in a good day's work. They can be derived from the journey itself, where the means are just as important as the ends. These internal rewards are available to us regardless of our position in life; we need only seek within and be true to ourselves.

Expand Your Horizons

For decades, higher education has performed a great disservice for many people. Today's colleges and universities are still following the century-old tradition of educating someone to achieve a single discipline or major field of study. This conservative educational process ignores the fact that all of us possess talents of multi-potentiality. We all are capable of being educated or skillfully trained in more than one discipline.

Each of us is capable of being successful in more than one career in life. If we go through college convinced that we can excel in only one discipline, we put on blinders and look for jobs centered only on this single major. Take off the blinders and expand your horizons. Take stock of all your skills, experiences, learning, growth, and maturation. With your family, friends, and networks of former classmates and colleagues, you become a distinctive person. A total picture of yourself emerges.

Learning: An Ongoing Process

As we venture through life, we are constantly making new discoveries about ourselves, the people who surround us and the world in which we live. When we cease to learn, we begin to stagnate. We must challenge ourselves so we can continue to grow and respond to life creatively. If we truly seek change, we need to be open to new learning and the development of new perceptions.

There is a certain degree of comfort in doing the same thing the same way every day. We encourage home and work routines, but unvarying structure can become a stifling rut. One of the easiest by-ways to start on the road to higher creativity and learning is to vary our daily routines. You can make changes with very little disruption and, at the same time, encourage a deeper awareness and broaden your spectrum of life experiences. Find a creative and unconventional way to respond to what you normally do, your likes, and your dislikes.

> Eliminate something superfluous from your life. Break a habit. Do something that makes you feel insecure.
> —*Piero Ferrucci*

When it comes to physical wellness, the locus of control for your body must be your own will-power and mindset, not that of anyone else, including all of the so-called "health gurus." Control of your lifestyle must be internal, not external. You alone can determine the personal lifestyle that you value and treasure. You must believe that you will succeed in whatever you choose to undertake. This internal conviction is a vital component of your decision to take charge of your own life and achieve personal well-being.

This take-charge attitude is immediate and within your reach. Do not wait until you reach the proverbial light at the end of the tunnel. The tunnel may be very long and the light at its end may not be what you are looking for. Are you aware that there is a light switch right next to you that can turn on the lights within the tunnel and help you find out clearly where you are and where you are going? There is no need to wait for fate or someone else to shine light into your life. It is within your reach right now. Turn it on and let it shine for yourself and others.

> The light is NOT at the end of the tunnel. It is inside the tunnel! And the switch is right next to you. TURN IT ON NOW!
> —*Phil Hwang*

One of the easiest by-ways to start on the road to creative responses in life is to alter your daily routine. Take a creative and unconventional response to what you normally do, to your likes and dislikes.

There is a certain degree of comfort in doing the same thing, the same way, everyday. You tend to encourage comfortable home and work routines, enjoying the ease of unvarying structure until those satisfying routines become stifling ruts. But you can make changes with very little disruption and, at the same time, encourage a deeper degree of awareness and broaden your spectrum of life experiences.

In addition, when we encounter new ideas and concepts, one of the best ways to internalize them is by teaching them to others. We all learn in different ways, so teaching someone something new may require you to look at the information in a way you had not thought of before. As a result, you develop a deeper and clearer understanding. Thus, teaching is not just a transfer of knowledge from you to your pupil, but a process of learning together.

Building Blocks for the By-Ways to Knowledge and Acceptance of Self and Others

- List attributes about yourself that you like. What contributions do you feel you make that are unique to you?
- List the unique attributes of the people in your Wheel of Intimates and Ring of Friendship. Share these with those people.
- Enjoy a new ethnic meal with someone from that culture. Then, relate this experience to a colleague or friend.
- Read a different magazine, journal, or newspaper than you usually read, and discuss it with someone who normally reads that particular magazine.
- Go with someone to a play, concert, or lecture you had never tried before, and share your experience with someone from your third ring of support.
- Watch a movie or TV program selected by someone else. Then, find something positive or meaningful to say about it.
- Ask some native speakers to teach you greetings in their native languages, and use them to greet them everyday.
- Travel to a foreign country with someone from that country. After your return home, share your experiences with students in schools; give a talk in a service club, etc.
- Attend a sporting event you've never been to with someone who is knowledgeable in a sport you don't know much about.
- List three behaviors that have been causing you and others around you unhappiness. Inform three of your circle of support and ask them to help you change.

2. The By-Way to Nurturing Self and Others

Taking Time for Self and Others

An important by-way of effecting positive change and caring for someone is spending time with them. This includes time for yourself. Give yourself permission to spend at least 10–15 minutes of quiet time each day to spend in personal self-reflection or meditation. This not only gives you a much-needed time out of the hectic pace of daily life; it also enables you to relax your mind. During this time, try to relax totally and do nothing. Spend this time totally alone without any distractions. A relaxing stint in a Jacuzzi or a bubble bath, lounging on a favorite chair, or simply lying in bed is ideal.

This personal time is needed every day to purge the stresses from the body and mind. These few moments should be considered vital nourishment for the inner self, just as food is vital nourishment for the body. Focusing on positive thoughts during this time and recalling happy moments and successes of the day will also encourage your new enthusiasm to grow and become a permanent part of your life. This may seem self-indulgent to some. You may feel there is so much to do, you cannot take time for yourself. But I am reminded of the importance of self-nurturing whenever I fly a commercial airline. The flight attendant always talks about what to do should emergency oxygen be necessary. In that safety speech, passengers are reminded that those traveling with children should fit their own oxygen masks first and then attend to their children. While this may seem backwards, it makes sense in that if the adults are incapacitated, they will be unable to do anything for anyone else.

So it is with personal time. Without a time to release the stresses of the day, they build up and we are less efficient, less effective, and less able to do with and for others. Unless we keep ourselves cared for and nurtured, we cannot truly nurture others. This does not mean we take care of ourselves only and not attend to anything or anyone else. It means that we need to become aware of our limitations and allow ourselves to take the time to revitalize and refresh daily so that we can more fully participate in life.

Just as it is important to make time for ourselves, it is equally important to make time to connect with others. With our busy schedules, it is easy to "cocoon" (as discussed in Chapter 5). But relationships must be nurtured to thrive, and this takes time and attention. A card, a phone call, or a lunch or dinner together are all connections with others that nurture them and are necessary for the health of our relationships.

Living Simply Benefits Everyone

An important step toward achieving emotional wellness both for us as individuals and as a planet is learning to live more simply. A look around our society immediately tells us that we are living a highly unrealistic lifestyle of striving toward improbable goals, both for ourselves and for others. This results in constant frustration.

We have too much of the good life in this country. We inherit individual freedom while people in other countries are dying for these rights. We consume natural resources in quantities far beyond the proportion of our population in the world. People who live or travel in third-world countries tend to cherish and treasure life in America. By living simply we learn to appreciate our opportunities and circumstances. The more we appreciate our lives, the brighter they become.

Rather than viewing life as a series of disposable items and material wants, we can make impressive strides toward preventing personal obsolescence and reducing environmental pollution by purchasing items that are built to last and are recyclable or biodegradable. We can even try our hands at repairing small products or finding someone who can fix them.

Most importantly, we must make a firm commitment never to view people or relationships as being disposable. Instead of a lot of "hello-goodbye" relationships, we can learn to concentrate and nurture a few important, close, and life-long relationships in our Circle of Intimates and Ring of Friendship. These are the people we support in the ups and downs of life and who support us as we go on our life's journey. Our families, those around us, our environment, and we personally will all benefit from this change in attitude and behavior. Our community as a whole will be better off.

Building Blocks for the By-Way to Nurturing Self and Others

- Make an appointment with yourself for quiet time alone. Schedule it in your calendar. Have a fixed time every day that is just for you. You could set the clock for 15 minutes earlier, go to bed 15 minutes later, take a walk at lunch, anything to set aside a small oasis of time for self.
- Let yourself experience all your senses. Walk barefoot on the grass or sand. Smell the flowers, the air, and even the people around you. Listen to some beautiful soothing music with your eyes closed to shut out all but the sounds. Taste something new.
- Once or twice a year, spend a weekend by yourself for reflection

and quiet time. At the same time, respect and support others' need for time to nurture themselves.

- Make appointments with members of your Circle of Intimacy and Ring of Friendship for time together. This needs your investment in terms of time, effort, and resources.
- Make it a point to contact one friend a week by phone, mail, e-mail, or in person. Remember, nurturing of others' demands investment in terms of time, effort, and even resources.
- Re-organize and re-focus your life. This should be reflected in some degrees of changes in your lifestyle habits and even in the cleaning and throwing away of clutter in a drawer, desk, closet, or room.
- Experts in time management say that things that you have not used for a year you probably don't need. Give to charity any items or clothing you have not used in the past year.
- Hold a day of honor for someone. Ask some friends and colleagues to honor someone who has served as a mentor or special friend and somehow made a difference in their lives. It needs not be elaborate. Prepare the honoree's special dish, and give each one present the opportunity to say a few words.
- Sarah Ban Breathnach (1995) suggests keeping a gratitude journal. Every night, write down five things about the day for which you are grateful. This helps keep your thoughts all night on the blessings in your life.
- Often be a support to others, especially when it is unsolicited.

3. The By-Way to Inner Peace and Harmony with Others

A next step to achieving emotional wellness and balance is to increase your level of tolerance for stress so you can more easily absorb the shocks that invariably occur in life and relationships. At work and in social and personal relationships, we must learn to reduce personal conflicts to more manageable levels. Each of us must find out what things bother us and why. It is the small irritations, seemingly insignificant at first, that grow persistently and blow us over.

Challenge your mental attitude by minimizing little irritations and letting petty annoyances be straws that roll off our back, not allowing them to build up to be a burdensome load that you carry around with you. You can also make great strides by resolving to clear the air daily of all conflicts and disagreements. The old cliché "never go to bed angry" is not only excellent advice for family solidarity, but will also guarantee us a much needed night's rest. We know that physical cleansing is a daily necessity; we can also perform a personal catharsis each day.

What about anger that is not minor? Medical experts have informed us that anger is a killer. It precipitates violence, the most destructive of all negative social behaviors. It affects the heart and diminishes our immune system's ability to ward off stresses and biological diseases. Many suggest physical exercise, sports, or hobbies for relaxation and stress reduction. These are essential elements of a healthy life. However, for many, they only act as Band-Aids.

Psychologists and other mental health workers often suggest that their clients "let off steam." The problem with releasing one's negative emotions is that there are too many variables affecting one's frustration. Uncontrolled negative release of emotion may not solve the problems that brought about the strong personal reaction, may actually reinforce the violent behavior of the individual, and may also provoke an equal opposing emotional reaction from the other person. However, controlled and directed release of these negative emotions, with the help of a professional if necessary, can reduced them to tolerable irritations of life or positive forces for effective change.

Building Blocks for the By-Way to Inner Peace and Harmony with Others

- Write down a list of things that annoy you. Rip them up or burn them and let them float away. Or visualize them each as pieces of straw that fall to the ground as you leave them behind.
- Make a list of things for which you have not forgiven yourself. Write an apology to yourself and forgive yourself in writing.
- Call at least two persons in your inner circle. Share with them and seek advice on how to forgive yourself and perhaps seek forgiveness. Ask them to share their story with you.
- Volunteer to give a talk on forgiveness to a class of school children.
- If you have issues of long-term anger or resentment, consider making an appointment with a professional to work on ridding yourself of this burden.
- List instances when you have tried to seek revenge in words or action during the last year.
- Express your sorrow and ask forgiveness from three different people you have hurt (little irritations or great pains) during the last year.
- Forgive those who have hurt you and, if possible, let them know that you forgive them.
- Develop an attitude and willingness to accept and let go of accidents or unexpected events of life that hurt you in ways you don't deserve.
- Promote world peace and speak out against discriminations and social injustices in your community.

4. The By-Way to a Life of Interdependency

Most of us want the best in life and have a desire to transform ourselves. Based on the principles of other-esteem discussed in these pages,
this transformation can be done best through mutual sharing and support. For this reason, we need the support and encouragement of
others close to us. Together we will take the road less traveled, and
the journey will be easier and brighter.

Learning to change together means sharing this special vision with
someone who is willing to see life from a different perspective. Find
people who will compliment, support, and promote each other. Each
of us possesses certain wonderful attributes as well as shortcomings.
Because we are unique we complement these attributes and shortcomings for one another. In life, we need all kinds of people. Together
we can do it. Alone we will fall short. There is no such thing as a self-
made person.

Intimacy: A Life of Togetherness

Life is better when shared with a significant someone. This does not
refer to marital status or living arrangements, but rather to a special
personal attachment and intimacy with another person. Healthy intimate relationships, romantic or otherwise, based on mutual respect,
love, caring, and support lighten our load and make us healthier and
happier.

This is a message for loners, for those who cannot or do not know
how to share themselves. Believe that there are people out there who
will appreciate you and benefit from the way you are. In return, you
will improve your quality of life. Happiness is multiplied when celebrated
with someone. Burdens are lightened when shared with others.

Building Blocks for the By-Way
to a Life of Interdependency

- Explain your new by-way path to those in your Circle of Intimates
  and Ring of Friendship. Solicit their support in helping you pave
  the by-way to meaningful life. At the same time, offer your support
  to help them build their own.
- Organize an "other-esteem" group to meet once a week or once a
  month to share your progress and support for one another.
- Ask three people from your inner circle or ring of friendship about
  their problems, dreams, and aspirations. And offer to be one of
  those in their own inner circle or ring or friendship. Finally, set a

six-month goal for you to help them in solving their problems and attaining their dreams and aspirations.

- Be vocal about alleviating injustices and discriminations you see around you. Take a stand and be part of the solution in your community.
- Make an extra effort to show kindness and respect to every person you come in contact with during your day. Thank the service people who wait on you.
- When you stay at hotels, make sure you leave a tip for the maids. Just because they are not there to thank you personally, you'd rather pocket the money. We all tip the porter who brings our luggage to our room? Why not the maids, who work harder than the porter, to clean up our messy room?
- Frequently express your humility in your dependence on others— your family, friends, colleagues, etc. Without them, there would not be a you today.
- Let those in your circle of intimacy know how much you value them. Write or call to thank them in a very personal way for being a very meaningful part of your life.
- Be present for others' moment of achievement and celebration. Show your love and care by attending these events or helping to support causes that they are involved in.
- Create a road map of the milestones in your life—achievements and disappointments. Next to each milestone, write down as many people as you can think of who helped or supported you in big and small ways at these times. How have you help or supported some of these people as they passed their milestones?

5. The By-Way to Friendship and Fellowship

Friendship: Synergy and Support

Miguel de Cervantes' words in *Don Quixote*, written in 1605, are just as appropriate today: "Tell me thy company, and I'll tell thee what thou art." If you want to be a positive, healthy and balanced person, you must learn to associate with positive, healthy, and balanced people. These are the people who radiate positive, enthusiastic, and dynamic energy. It is exciting to search for those people who will support and encourage us and offer great enthusiasm for our undertakings.

Just as enthusiasm and positive thinking can influence those around us, so can a negative and defeatist attitude. There are two things to do when faced with negative or critical people. First of all, learn from them! Understand their experiences and try to see things from their perspective. Learn what you ought to avoid and what you need to do to prevent yourself from becoming one of them. Demonstrate your other-esteem and hope to promote some changes in them.

But sometimes you must simply disassociate yourself from them. Spending time with negative people will only bring you down to their level. The old adage "misery loves company" is an accurate reflection of their outlook. Doom-and-gloom people do not like to see others happy and positive, and they will not be satisfied until you are just as negative and defeatist as they are. Just as joy, cheer, and enthusiasm are contagious, so, unfortunately, is a doom-and-gloom attitude.

We must protect ourselves by associating with people who have a positive outlook on life. Discovering people who are willing to help, who believe in us, and who will offer assistance without expecting payment in return will catapult us to new emotional and intellectual heights. By having such people as role models, we can begin to understand their perspectives and approaches to life, and apply them to our own lives. We may not be aware of it, but winners are all around us—among our neighbors, friends, and colleagues—ready to help improve our attitude. Search them out. Join up with them. Invite them into your Ring of Friendship. Their support will magnify the positive results, and will give a great boost to your attitude and your life.

Each of us has unique perspectives and insights to offer. If we support one another and work together, meeting life's challenges—both small and large—becomes easier and much less overwhelming. If we always face life alone, it is easy to develop tunnel vision and only see one approach to problem solving. But when we work together, a synergy develops that allows us to discover more creative solutions.

Suppose your child is having academic difficulty in high school. She thinks the only solution is to drop out; from her perspective, no other solution is possible. You, on the other hand, can think of several options in the blink of an eye: professional tutors, special classes, teacher assistance, peer tutoring programs, and so on. Your experience allows you to be more creative and decisive in your explorations, and this in turn will teach your child that there are always more solutions than are first apparent.

The same attitude also works well with relationships, within the family and in the workplace. There is always more than one way to resolve a situation. You are only limited by your creativity, imagination, and willingness to explore new areas and concepts. The answers are found inside each of us, sometimes with the help of the people around us. We can help one another discover our own answers and support one another in our search.

Community: Responsibility to One Another

In today's multicultural society, human rights and social justice are extremely important for us all. Perhaps we can find a way to better balance our rights and responsibilities. Life is more meaningful when it is shared with others. Look around the communities in which you live, work, and play. What do you want to protect for your community? What would you like to change? How can you contribute? We are each responsible for helping to make our communities what they are. Our actions (or inaction) as individuals affect not only ourselves, but also others who live and work around us.

The need for each of us to become involved and help build a better life for all is extremely vital in a diverse society. There is a need for advocates who are willing to challenge the status quo and take up the causes of the discriminated, the less privileged, the less able in all facets of our society.

Building Blocks for the By-Way to Friendship and Fellowship

- Offer to be a support for at least three people in their programs of wellness as well as in physical, emotional, and spiritual growth and development.
- Volunteer in a program in your community that has meaning to you. Help clean up in a recycling program, mentor a child through Big Brothers or Big Sisters, help children in an after-school tutoring program, teach an adult to read, or read to an elderly patient in a nursing home. Find a way to give to your community and spend time outside of yourself.
- Write or call to thank three different people for their positive contributions to your life. Be specific on how they have impacted your life. Offer to become part of their support system.
- Volunteer to become an advocate for some less privileged group. Attend their meetings; learn all you can about this group and offer to be a speaker to various civic groups on their behalf.
- Ask three different people from your ring of support to listen to some of your concerns, visions, and projects. Ask them for support to help you alleviate some of your problems and help fulfill your vision and dreams.
- Develop your tolerance for others, especially when driving. Give them the smile and wave of hand instead of the half-peace sign.
- Friendship is an attitude of mind. Be ready to help when asked.
- Ask some of your friends about their personal vision of life, and in your own way offer to help them fulfill their vision.

- Traffics, lines, delays, etc. are all gifts of time. Be ready to accept these gifts with gratitude and respond creatively. Think not only out of the box, but think without the box.
- Experts say that you have to accept what you can't change, and change what you can. But can we learn to change with others' help?

6. The By-Way to Leadership and "Followship"

Our competitive society teaches us to be Number One all the time. Winning is everything. Being the best, biggest, largest, and Number One are all frequently heard labels. Certain competition in life is healthy and productive. Sports by their very nature are competitive, and there are definite winners and losers. Thousands of spectators enjoy and have fun at these functions. Others maintain their physical health through competitive, recreational events. It is wonderful to win and may be depressing to lose, but it is all part of life and just a game.

The sad part is that many of us transfer this competitiveness and this need or desire to win to areas other than sporting events. In the arena of human relations, it is not healthy to strive for the upper hand. In the corporate world, teamwork should be stressed over individual accomplishments. There should not be any win-lose competition, not even the deceptive win-win substitute. It is okay to lose, to be Number Two, or to be a follower.

Dr. Rudolph Dreikurs, a famous Adlerian Psychotherapist, said, "We should all have our second child first." All of us want to be young, strong, powerful, and wealthy. Many of us are very uncomfortable with the thought of being in a powerless position; thus, we seek positions of power in every avenue possible. Most people who accumulate wealth do so not only for the sake of money, but also (and most importantly), for the power that comes with wealth.

In western culture, money represents power and control. It may frighten us to see others we know acquire more money—and thus more power—than we have. Therefore, we seek to control to avoid being controlled by others, and seek to manipulate to avoid being manipulated by others. Everyone should ask, "Does being second best place you in a powerless position?" I firmly believe that you can be just as happy being number two. Most of the time, being number one entails many sacrifices and costs, and those who deem themselves number one do not seem much happier to me. Being the second-born rather than the traditional hard-working first-born who competes with everyone has its own rewards. In life, we play various roles in different situations. Sometimes we experience leadership roles; other times we learn how to follow the lead of others. There is absolutely no need to be the top banana always.

Rather than always struggling to top each other, we must learn to work together, and to promote and care for one another. Denis, Dayna and Deborah Waitley redefine winning in an other-esteem-focused way. They talk about winning as "living your life successfully, based on what you want to achieve—being your best instead of the best. It's your own personal pursuit of individual excellence. You don't have to get lucky or knock down other people or profit at someone else's expense" (1999, p. 18). By their definition, winning means helping others to win too. In this sense, we are always leaders and followers. Sometimes we show the way; sometimes we lead by helping others become leaders; sometimes we support by following other people's leadership.

Building Blocks for the By-Way to Leadership and "Followship"

- Be a mentor to someone with whom you work. Leadership is caring for others. A mentor is a coach; you want the best to happen to your "mentee."
- Seek ideas about improving your performance at work from your boss, colleagues, and direct reports. Thank them, give them credit for those ideas, and ask them to continue on a quarterly basis.
- Actively seek out and openly compliment the successes of other co-workers. Be among the first to support and promote their accomplishments.
- Build and nurture your network of personal and professional contacts within and outside your organization.
- Be part of someone's network. Look daily for ways to be a link for others to connect to one another.
- Learn what your company's vision is and promote that vision in the work you do.
- Make a vision statement for your own life. Share it with selected colleagues who will support you. Frame it and put it up on your office wall.
- If you are in a leadership position, choose to listen and follow others' suggestions at least once a day.
- Practice asking for help or directions and be ready to be just as helpful to others.
- Leaders should facilitate and not mitigate. If you are a leader, find ways to help your direct reports map out the career paths and fulfill the dreams of those you lead.

☐ Start Today!

Let's start our new life with others today. Today, a happier, unconventional, and different you evolves. You have learned to see the
world anew. This learning will transform you immediately, and eventually spread to those around you. This metamorphosis is a movement
from focusing on the self to finding a balance and harmonious coming
together of the self and other.

Today, you set foot down a new path, the by-ways to a meaningful
life in a multicultural society. You expect the best from yourself and
from those around you. You are willing to give as you are willing to
receive. You are optimistic about the future because you have a group
of wonderful people within your circle of support to help you. With
them, you can take on the world.

Today, you are ready to show your new attitude toward yourself,
others, and life. Esteem those with whom you are intimate. Esteem
friends, acquaintances, and even strangers, who may think, feel, and
act differently from you.

Today, you expand your perception to include a global perspective
of life and work. Share yourself with others in a mutual commitment
to a vision of life based on other-esteem.

Today, you are ready to share yourself. As the saying goes, "Life is
like a lighted candle. When you light another candle, you share yourself, but your light stays the same. There is not less of your light. But
together there is more light to see." Let your light shine.

REFERENCES

Aurelius, Marcus. *Meditations* V 16.

Baumeister, R. F., Boden, J. M., & Smart, L. (1996). Relation of threatened egotism to violence and aggression: The dark side of self-esteem. *Psychological Review, 103,* 5–29.

Begley, S. (1998, July 13). You're OK, I'm terrific: "Self-esteem" Backfires. *Newsweek,* 69.

Blanchard, K. (1982). *The one minute manager.* New York: Morrow.

Bradshaw, J. (1996). *Bradshaw on the Family: A new way of creasing solid self-esteem.* Deerfield Beach, Florida: Health Communications.

Breathnach, S. B. (1995) *Simple Abundance: A daybook of comfort and joy.* New York: Warner Books.

Carnegie, D. (1936). *How to win friends and influence people.* New York: Simon Schuster.

Covey, S. R. (1989). *The seven habits of highly effective people.* New York: Simon and Schuster.

Ferrucci, P. (1990). *Inevitable grace.* Los Angeles: Jeremy P. Tarcher.

Flaubert, C. L. (1997). *Eight habits of the heart: Embracing the values that build strong families and communities.* New York: Viking Press.

Frankl, V. (1984). *Man's search for meaning.* New York. Simon & Schuster.

Frost, Robert. (1995). "Haec Fabula Docet." *Frost: Collected poems, prose and plays.* New York: Library of Congress.

Greene, G. (1992). *The human factor.* New York. Random House.

Gawain, S. (1986). *Living in the light.* Mill Valley, CA: Whatever Publishing.

Kaplan, L. S. (1995). Self-esteem is not our national wonder drug. *School Counselor, 42,* 341.

MacIntyre, A (1984). *After virtue: A study in moral theory.* Notre Dame: Ind. University of Notre Dame Press.

Naisbett, J. (1982). *Megatrends: Ten new directions transforming our lives.* New York: Warner Books.

Ornish, D. (1998). *Love and survival: The scientific basis for the healing power of intimacy.* New York: Harpercollins.

Rachels, J. (1986). *The elements of moral philosophy.* Philadelphia: Temple University Press.

Rosenbluth, H. F. (1994). *The customer comes second and other secrets of exceptional service.* New York: Morrow.

Seligman, M. E. P. (1991). *Learned optimism: How to change your mind and your life.* New York: A. A. Knopf.

Stevenson, R. L. (1905) is from *An inland voyage: Travels with a donkey in Edinburgh.* New York: Scribners.

Sullivan, W. (1982). *Reconstructing public philosophy.* Berkeley, CA: University of California Press.

The self-esteem fraud: Feeling good does not lead to academic success. (1998, January). *USA Today, 126,* 66.

Waitley, Denis, Deborah, Dayna. (1999). *The psychology of winning for women.* Provo: The Waitley Institute.

Weissbourd, R. (1996, August 19). The feel-good trap. *The New Republic, 216,* 12.

ABOUT THE AUTHOR

Dr. Philip O. Hwang is Professor and Director of the Counseling Program at University of San Diego. He has been at USD since 1974 and has held numerous teaching and administrative duties, including Director of Doctoral Program in Leadership, Director of Marriage, Family, and Child Counseling, and Director of School Counseling programs. In 1977, Dr. Hwang was named "Outstanding Teacher of the Year" by the University of San Diego.

Professor Hwang is an extremely popular and dynamic speaker, consultant, and lecturer. He is a specialist in Group Dynamics. He also lectures and conduct seminars on Stress Management, Assertiveness Training, Psychology of Forgiveness, Effective Leadership Training, Organizational Change, and Multiculturalism. He has given numerous keynote addresses and speeches before conventions, service organizations, churches, schools, and government agencies.

Dr. Hwang has personal passion for internationalism and a keen interest in diverse cultures. He has escorted numerous educational and cultural tours to China, Hong Kong, Russia, Australia, New Zealand, Hungary, and Yugoslavia. He believes that the best way to acquire a higher level of understanding, respect, and acceptance of others (and thus other-esteem), is through personal experience of one another's culture.

INDEX

Page references in italics indicate a figure or illustration.

Abusive relationships, silent conspiracy of, 43–55
Accidents of birth and life, 107–108
After Virtue (MacIntyre), 53
American culture
  confidentiality practices of, 45, 46–47
  contrast to Asian culture, 112–114
  disposable relationships, 59–60, 65–68
  as fast food society, 9–11
  focus on self and independence, 1–22
  focus on short-term in business, 89–91
  forgiveness viewed as a weakness, 125
  ignorance of interdependency, 36
  immediate gratification, 7–9
  prevalence of silence, 46–47
  self-importance as learning block, 6–7
  stoic individualism, 5–7

Bad luck, 30–31
Baumeister, R. F., 3, 14
Beck, Aaron, 27
Belief systems
  balance of culture and traditions, 110–114
  as facet of other–esteem, 17, 18*f*, 19*f*, 20*f*
  sorting irrational and rational beliefs, 35–36
Ben and Jerry's Company, vision statement of, 93

Big Mac Syndrome, The, 9–11
Blanchard, Ken, 100
Boden, J. M., 3
Bradshaw, John, 34–35
Brainwashing and belief systems, 35–36
Breathnach, Sarah Ban, 152
Business
  bottom line vs. consequences, 95–97
  communication and feedback, 100–101, 102*f*, 103*f*, 104–106
  diversity program of recruitment, 117–119
  focus on short-term, 89–91
  "followship" as step toward a meaningful life, 158–159
  future-oriented vision of, 92–94, 120–121
  "Hello-Goodbye" attitude, 91–92
  interdependency of colleagues, 98–100
  mentoring process for retention, 119, 159
  mutual commitment of workers, 94–97
  networking internally and externally, 104–106, 120–121
  "self–made millionaire," reality of, 98–100
  team player synergy, 94–98
By-ways to a meaningful life, 143–145, 145*f*, 146–160

Carnegie, Dale, 28
Change
  possibilities in relationships, 64–65

Change (*Cont.*):
  recognition of unchangeable and
    changeable events, 36–38, 38*f,*
    39*f*
  self-importance as a block, 6–7
Checklist for other-esteem, 20*f*
Childhood and family, impact on
    personality and outlook, 34–36
Choices, options of, 30–32
Chu, Chin-Ning, 77
Circles of Support, 35–36, 69–70, 69*f,*
    71, 86–88
Co-conspirators, reasons for secrecy,
    49–50
"Cocooning," 81–82, 150
Cognition, definition of, 27
Cognitive distortions
  of community and self, 84–85
  of love, 58–59, 61–63
  vs. thinking, 26–38, 38*f,* 39*f,* 40*f,*
    41*f*
Cognitive Therapy, 27–28
Communication and feedback, in work
    environment, 100–101, 104
Community
  fellowship as step toward a meaning-
    ful life, 157–158
  importance in relationships, 6–7,
    84–88
  networking with business, 104–106
Competition, presence in multicultural
    society, 109
Confidentiality in society, 45–47
Control, healthy balance of, 32–34,
    36
Coping mechanisms, impact on
    attitudes and perceptions, 28
Cultural discrimination, origins of,
    29–30
Culture and traditions, balance in belief
    systems, 110–114

Destructive Phase of Forgiveness, 135–
    138, 141*f,* 142*f*
Discrimination
  and exaggerated self-esteem, 108–
    109
  origins of, 29–30
Disposable relationships, 59–60
Distorted view of life's events, 37–38
Dreikurs, Rudolph, 158

Earned self-esteem, 4
Elements of Moral Philosophy, The
    (Rachels), 53
Ellis, Albert, 27, 34
Emotional drunkards, 35–36
Ethical considerations and conse-
    quences of actions, 25–26
Ethnic warfare, origins of, 29–30
Excuses of life's events, 38*f,* 39*f*
Expectations of self and others, 76–79

Family
  as facet of other-esteem, 57–63, 63*f,*
    64–70, 69*f,* 71
  impact on personality in outlook,
    34–36
Fast food vs. dining socialization, 9–11
Fast Instant Relief Syndrome (FIRES),
    7–9, 80, 89, 91
Feedback and communication in work
    environment, 100–101, 104
FIRES (Fast Instant Relief Syndrome),
    7–9, 80, 89, 91
Followers and leaders, interdependency
    of, 20–22
Forgiveness
  benefit of, 125, 126, 129–130
  as constructive behavior, 132
  living for the future, 124–126
  minor irritations and "last straw,"
    130–131
  phases of, 133–139, 141*f,* 142*f*
  principles of, 126–132
  psychology of, 19*f,* 123–141, 141*f,*
    142*f*
  rationales for unforgiveness, 124–
    126
  supporting others, 140
Frankl, Victor, 23–24
Freedom, personal, 11–14
Friendship, Ring of, 73–74, 74*f,* 75–85,
    85*f,* 87*f,* 86–88
Friendships
  expectations of self and others, 77–
    79
  factors affecting depth of, 74–84
  "Hello-Goodbye" friendships, 79–80
  mutual sharing of self, 75–76, 82–84
  as step toward meaningful life, 155–
    158
Fung Shi, 30–31

Future
in business vision, 92–94, 120–121
essential to healing and world peace,
124–126

Gawain, Shakti, 53
Global networking, 105–106, 120–121
Global shrinking, impact of technology,
4, 29–30, 105–106
Gnossos Software diversity program,
118
Goals
convergence of social and individual,
16
Good fortune, 30–31
Gratitude journal for personal time,
152
Greene, Graham, 116

Happiness, impact on perceptions,
28
Harmony and inner peace, step toward
meaningful life, 34, 150–152
Healing Phase of Forgiveness, 138–139,
141f, 142f
Healing, psychology of, 123–141, 141f,
142f
"Hello-Goodbye"
business relationships, 91–92
friendships, 79–80
marriages and divorces, 59–60
Hero-worshipping in American culture,
7
Human Factor, The, (Greene), 116
Human Potentials, 1
Humans
fragility of body and soul, 78
reality of limits, 28–29, 76–79

Immediate gratification, American
focus on, 7–9
"Imperfect perfection," 77
Independence, American focus on,
1–22
Individual Sensitivity Training, 1
Individualism, American reverence for,
5–7, 11–14
Inner peace and harmony, step toward
meaningful life, 152–153

Interdependency
American culture ignorance of, 36
establishing other-esteem, 15–17,
18f, 19f, 20, 20f, 21–22
and global shrinking, 29–30
and healthy balance of control,
32–34
impact on depth of friendships,
82–85
of leaders and followers, 20–22
principle of, 14
as step toward meaningful life,
154–155
teaching children relationship
essentials, 68–69
Interpretations of life events and
other-esteem, 24–38, 38f, 39f,
40f, 41f
Intimacy as step toward a meaningful
life, 57–63, 63f, 64–70, 69f, 71,
154
Intimacy, Inner Ring of, 57–63, 63f,
64–70, 69f, 71, 86–88
Irritations of life, 41f

Jurassic Park and ethical considerations,
25

Kaplan, L. S., 4

Leadership
"followship" as step toward a
meaningful life, 158–159
future-oriented vision of, 92–94
"Hello-Goodbye Business" attitudes,
91–92, 101, 102f, 103f, 104
interdependency with followers,
20–22
Loop Paradigm model for, 92–101,
102f, 103f, 104–106
Learning
as growing process toward meaningful life, 147–149
positive use of mistakes, 35–36
teaching children relationship
essentials, 68–69
Life's events
distorted view of, 37–38
human life as series of relationships,
75

Life's events (*Cont.*):
  interpretation of, 34–38, 38*f,* 39*f,* 40*f,* 41*f*
  recognition of unchangeable and changeable events, 36–38, 38*f,* 39*f*
Listening as facet of other-esteem, 22
Loop Paradigm model of organizational relationships, 92–101, 102*f,* 103*f,* 104–106
Love
  as facet of other-esteem, 62–63
  myth and fantasy about, 58–59, 61–63
Low self-esteem and social problems, 2–3

MacIntyre, Alasdir, 53
Majority groups, rights of, 114–117
Man's Search for Meaning (Frankl), 23–24
"Me" generation and self-esteem, 14
Meaningful life, byways to, 143–145, 145*f,* 146–160
Megatrends (Naisbett), 84
Mental attitudes
  cognitive distortions of, 26–27
  as facet of other-esteem, 17, 18*f,* 19*f,* 20*f,* 24–38, 38*f,* 39*f,* 40*f,* 41*f*
  forgiveness as a choice, 129, 131–132
  possibilities for change in relationships, 64–65
Minds, power of, 27–28
Minority groups, rights of, 114–119
Mobile lifestyle, impact on depth of friendships, 80–81
Morality and silent conspiracy, 52–53
Movements
  assertiveness training, 1
  of self-esteem, 1–5
Multicultural societies, possibilities with other-esteem, 107–121
Mutual dependency, establishing other-esteem, 15–17, 18*f,* 19*f,* 20, 20*f,* 21–22
Mutual need in partnerships, 75–76, 82–84

Naisbett, John, 84
Negative behaviors
  communication and feedback, 100–101
  as learning experience, 35–36
  reinforcement with secrecy, 46–47
Networking in the work environment, 104–106, 120–121

One Minute Manager (Blanchard), 100
Optimism as facet of other-esteem, 27–28
Organizational relationships, Loop Paradigm model of, 92–101, 102*f,* 103*f,* 104–106
Other and Self
  balance of, 17, 21, 22, 109–114
  concept of others, 15–16
  expectations of, 77–78

Painful Phase of Forgiveness, 133–135, 141*f,* 142*f*
Perceptions
  irrational vs. rational belief system, 35–36
  of life's events, 34–38, 38*f,* 39*f,* 40*f,* 41*f*
  sharing of, 35–36
Perfection, expectations and reality of humans, 28–29, 76–79
Personal and social responsibilities, 2–3
  balance of personal and other rights, 113
  balance with self-centeredness, 11–14
  breaking the silence of secrecy, 46–55
  establishing "other-esteem," 15–17, 18*f,* 19*f,* 20, 20*f,* 21–22
Personal freedom, cognitive distortions vs. thinking, 26–27
Personal intimacy as facet of other-esteem, 57–63, 63*f,* 64–70, 69*f,* 71, 154
Personal time for nurturing self and others, 150–152
Personal wellness training program, 144
Person-centered therapy, 46–47
Philippines, impact of American occupation, 114
Positive attitudes, facet of other-esteem, 27–28

Promote Self-Esteem and Personal and
    Social Responsibility (State of
    California), 2

Rachels, James, 53
Racial discrimination, origins of, 29–30
Rational Emotive Therapy, 34
Rational view of life's events, 37–38
Reality
    of human limits, 28–29, 76–79
    and sharing of perceptions, 35–36
Reconstructing Public Philosophy
    (Sullivan), 53
Relationships
    commitment and personal sacrifice
        of, 61–63, 65–68
    competitive marriages, 65–66
    and disposable humans, 59–60
    as enriching experiences, 63–64
    fast food vs. dining socialization, 9–11
    "Hello-Goodbye" marriages/divorces,
        59–60
    importance of community, 84–88
    interdependency of, 82–85
    and intimate connections, 57–63,
        63f, 64–70, 69f, 71
    mutual need in partnerships, 75–76,
        82–84
    myth about love, 58–59, 61–63
    other-esteem in business and work,
        89–101, 102f, 103f, 104–106
    personal checklist of, 63f
    possibilities for change, 64–65
    retirement and friendships, 66
    Ring of Friendship support system,
        73–74, 74f, 75–85, 85f, 87f, 86–
        88
    teaching children relationship
        essentials, 68–69
Respect as facet of other-esteem, 17,
    18f, 19f, 20f, 34
Responsibility
    speaking out against crime, 46–55
    See also Personal and social
        responsibilities
Revenge, correlation with forgiveness,
    126–128
Ring of Friendship support system, 73–
    74, 74f, 75–85, 85f, 87f, 86–88
Ring of Intimacy, Inner, 57–63, 63f,
    64–70, 69f, 71, 86–88

Road rage and personal freedom, 23–24
Rogers, Carl, 46–47
Romantic love, myth and fantasy
    about, 58–59, 61–63

Secrecy
    co-conspiracy vs. speaking out, 49–
        54, 54f, 55
    confidentiality in society, 45, 46–47
    conspiracy of, 43–44, 44f, 45–54, 54f,
        55
    fear of retaliation, 49–53
    as negative behavior reinforcement,
        46–47
    social norms of, 44f
    unwilling co-conspirators, 49–54,
        54f, 55
Self
    expectations of, 77–78
    promotion of, 1–22
Self and Other
    balance of, 17, 21, 22, 109–114
    concept of others, 15–16
    expectations of, 77–78
    knowledge and acceptance step
        toward meaningful life, 145f,
        146–149
    nurturing self and others step toward
        meaningful life, 150–152
Self-centeredness, balance with social
    responsibility, 11–14
Self-control, 14
Self-esteem
    balance with other-esteem, 109–114
    definition of, 2
    and discrimination, 108–109
    earned, 4
    global, 4
    and "me" generation, 14
    movement of, 1–5
    and social problems, 2–3
Self-sufficiency, American focus on,
    1–22, 80
Sexual discrimination, origins of,
    29–30
Shanghai Psychiatric Hospital, 113–114
Silence
    conspiracy of, 43–44, 44f, 45–54, 54f,
        55
    speaking out against, 46–54, 54f, 55
Smart, L., 3

Sports
  hero-worshipping, 7
  team vs. individual motivations,
    12–13
Stereotypes, origins of, 29–30
Strengths and weaknesses, 34
Sullivan, William, 53
Superiority, sense of, 3
Support, Circles of, 69–70, 69f, 71,
  86–88
Syndromes
  Big Mac Syndrome, 9–11
  Fast Instant Relief Syndrome
    (FIRES), 7–9, 80, 89, 91
Synergy
  definition of, 97
  of teamwork, in business and work,
    95–97

Technology, impact on relationships,
  76–77, 105–106
Thick Face, Black Heart (Chu), 77
Time, American fixation on, 7–9
Tolerance as facet of other-esteem,
  17, 18f, 19f, 20f
Tolerance facet of other-esteem,
  29–30

Valuing as facet of other-esteem, 17,
  18f, 19f, 20f
Vietnam, impact of French rule,
  114
Violence, and levels of self-esteem,
  2–3, 4

Waitley, Dayna, 159
Waitley, Deborah, 159
Waitley, Denis, 159
Weight loss and control of life, 32–34
Weissbourd, R., 4
"What's in it for me" phenomenon,
  83–84
Wheel of Meaningful Life, The, 145,
  145f, 146–160
Work environment
  bottom line vs. consequences, 95–97
  communication and feedback, 100–
    101, 104
  diversity program of recruitment,
    117–119
  effects of other-esteem, 89–101,
    102f, 103f, 104–106
  focus on short-term, 89–91
  "followship" as step toward a
    meaningful life, 158–159
  future-oriented vision of, 92–94,
    120–121
  "Hello-Goodbye Business" attitude
    of, 91–92
  interdependency of colleagues, 98–
    100
  Loop Paradigm model of organiza-
    tional relationships, 92–101,
    102f, 103f, 104–106
  mentoring process for retention, 119,
    159
  mutual commitment of workers, 91–
    97
  networking internally and externally,
    104–106, 120–121
  team player synergy, 94–98